Mama Doris's Old-Fashioned

HOME COOKIN' RECIPES

SWEETWATER
PRESS

Mama Doris's Old-Fashioned Home Cookin' Recipes

Produced by Cliff Road Books

ISBN-13: 978-1-58173-591-8
ISBN-10: 1-58173-591-X

Design by Miles G. Parsons

Printed in China

Mama Doris's Old-Fashioned

HOME COOKIN' RECIPES

SWEETWATER
PRESS

CONTENTS

Mama Doris Always was the Best Cook in Town...

You could always count on Mama Doris to have something good cooking in her kitchen. The best biscuits in the morning, the best veggies for lunch, and the best steak and gravy for dinner. Not to mention cakes and pies that make you want to weep for joy. Mama Doris could cook anything. If you needed to know how to make something, she was the one to ask. She taught whole generations how to cook.

For more than fifty years, Mama cooked and kept a drawer full of her best recipes. From everyday basics to the fancy stuff. Now that good cookin' has been gathered into this book for you to enjoy with your family. It'll impress company, too. Guaranteed to please everyone at your table and definitely worth passing down to the next generation, 'cause they don't cook like this any more.

SOUPS

Soup Stock

2 to 3 pounds bone and meat
3 quarts water
sprig of parsley
1 onion, diced
stalk of celery and leaves
1 or 2 carrots, diced
1 or 2 bay leaves
4 cloves
6 peppercorns
salt to taste

Cut the meat into small pieces. Pour cold water over the meat and bones, using about 1 quart for each pound of meat. Add remaining ingredients and simmer gently in a covered pot for about 3 hours. The froth that rises to the top during the first part of the cooking time should be skimmed off. When soup stock is cool, it should be placed in the refrigerator until it is used. The fat will rise to the top and form a protective covering. If part of the stock is used, the fat should be removed and heated with the remaining stock so that it will always have the protective covering of fat.

Beef Stew with Dumplings

1-1/2 pounds lean beef, cut into 1-inch pieces
2-1/4 teaspoons salt, divided
1/8 teaspoon pepper
3 tablespoons flour
3 tablespoons butter
4 cups water
1/2 teaspoon hot sauce
12 small white onions, peeled
6 medium carrots, peeled and quartered
1-1/2 cups sifted flour
2 teaspoons baking powder
3/4 cup milk

Roll pieces of meat in mixture of 1/2 teaspoon salt, pepper, and flour. Melt butter in a heavy pot or dutch oven. Over medium-high heat, brown beef on all sides. Add water, 1/2 teaspoon salt, and hot sauce. Reduce heat. Cover and simmer for 2 hours, or until meat is almost tender. Add 1/2 teaspoon salt, onions, and carrots. Cover and cook until vegetables are tender. For dumplings, sift together flour, baking powder, and 3/4 teaspoon salt. Add milk; stir only until blended. Drop by spoonfuls into stew. Cook uncovered for 10 minutes. Cover tightly and simmer 10 minutes longer. Makes 6 to 8 servings.

Dried-Bean or Split-Pea Soup

1 cup dried beans or green or yellow split peas
1 small onion, diced
salt
4 tablespoons butter or margarine
4 tablespoons flour
1 quart milk

Soak beans or peas overnight in cold water. Add onions and salt, and cook until soft. Put through a sieve. Melt the butter in a medium saucepan over medium-high heat. Whisk in flour and cook, stirring constantly, for 3 to 4 minutes. Gradually add milk, whisking constantly to avoid lumps. Cook and stir until thick and bubbly. Add the peas and cook until well mixed.

Peanut Butter Soup

1 tall can evaporated milk
4 tablespoons butter
1 tablespoons flour
1/2 cup peanut butter
salt

Dilute the milk with an equal quantity of water. Melt the butter in a medium saucepan over medium-high heat. Whisk in flour and cook, stirring constantly, for 3 to 4 minutes. Gradually add milk, whisking constantly to avoid lumps. Cook and stir until thick and bubbly. Stir in the peanut butter and cook for a few minutes longer. Season with salt to taste.

Oatmeal Chowder

2 tablespoons butter
1 large onion, diced
3 cooked carrots, diced
1 cup split peas, cooked
2 cups tomatoes, chopped
2 cups cooked oatmeal
1 quart water
salt to taste

Melt the butter, add the onion, and cook until browned. Add all other ingredients and cook for 20 minutes.

Cream of Potato Soup

4 medium potatoes
1 quart milk
1/2 medium onion
2 tablespoons butter or margarine
1 teaspoon salt
1/8 teaspoon pepper

Peel and dice the potatoes. Cook in a small amount of boiling water until tender. Mash. Scald the milk and onion in a double boiler. Strain out the onion and add the milk, butter, salt, and pepper to the potatoes and reheat. One-quarter pound raw chopped kale, spinach, watercress, parsley, or similar green maybe added to the soup just before serving.

Cream of Celery Soup

3 cups celery
2 cups boiling water
4 tablespoons butter or margarine
4 tablespoons flour
2 cups milk
1/8 teaspoon pepper
1/2 teaspoon salt

Wash the celery and cut into pieces, using both stalk and leaves. Cook in a small amount of boiling water until very soft and tender; rub through a sieve. Melt the butter in a medium saucepan over medium-high heat. Whisk in flour and cook, stirring constantly, for 3 to 4 minutes. Gradually add milk, whisking constantly to avoid lumps. Cook and stir until thick and bubbly. Add to celery mixture; stir well. Season with salt and pepper.

Cream of Tomato Soup

2 cups tomato, seeded and chopped
1 onion, sliced
2 teaspoons sugar
2 cups milk
4 tablespoons butter
4 tablespoons flour
1 teaspoon salt
pepper

Cook tomatoes, onion, and sugar for about 5 minutes. Strain. Melt the butter in a medium saucepan over medium-high heat. Whisk in flour and cook, stirring constantly, for 3 to 4 minutes. Gradually add milk, whisking constantly to avoid lumps. Cook and stir until thick and bubbly. Add strained tomatoes slowly, stirring constantly. Season with salt and pepper and serve.

Corn Chowder

1 piece salt pork
1 onion, sliced
4 potatoes cut in 1/4-inch slices
2 cups boiling water
1 quart milk
2 cups fresh corn cut from the cob
salt and pepper

Cut pork into small pieces and fry it in a pan over low heat. Add the sliced onion and cook for 5 minutes. Strain the fat into a saucepan. Add the potatoes and 2 cups of boiling water to the fat and cook until the potatoes are soft. Then add the milk, cooked onion, and corn. Cook until boiling. Season with salt and pepper.

Fish Chowder

1 piece salt pork
1 onion, sliced
6 potatoes, cut into cubes
2 cups boiling water
2 cups flaked cod, fresh or frozen
1 quart milk
1 tablespoon salt
1/8 teaspoon pepper

Cut pork into small pieces and fry it in a pan over low heat. Add the sliced onion and cook until light brown. Strain the fat into a saucepan, add the potatoes and boiling water, and cook for 10 minutes. Add the fish and simmer for 20 minutes. Add the milk and seasonings. Heat to the boiling point and serve. Any white fish, oysters, or clams may be used in place of the codfish.

Chili con Carne

1 onion, minced
1 garlic clove
2 tablespoons bacon fat
1 pound ground beef
2 cups kidney beans, cooked or canned
2 cups tomatoes
1 teaspoon salt
pepper
1/2 teaspoon chili powder

Brown the onion and garlic in fat. Remove the garlic and discard. Add the meat and brown slightly. Add beans, tomatoes, and seasonings. Put in a greased baking dish or casserole. Bake at 350° for about 30 minutes. Makes 6 servings. The mixture may also be cooked at low temperature on top of the stove until thickened. The pan should be covered for the first part of the cooking.

Chicken Stew

3 pounds chicken
2 tablespoons vegetable oil
1/2 small onion, sliced
1 bay leaf
2 stalks of celery
1 carrot, sliced
1/2 teaspoon pepper
2 teaspoons salt

Cut chicken into serving pieces, then rinse and drain. Brown chicken in hot oil; cover with boiling water. Add onion, bay leaf, celery, carrot, and pepper. After 30 minutes, add salt and cook 15 more minutes.

Oyster Stew

1 quart oysters
1 quart milk
1/4 cup butter or fortified margarine
2 teaspoons salt
1/2 teaspoon pepper

Remove the oysters from the liquor, and pick them over carefully to remove any pieces of the shell. Strain the liquor into a saucepan and bring to simmer. Add the oysters and simmer gently until the edges begin to curl. Scald the milk, then add it along with the butter and seasonings.

Using It All Turkey Soup

1 turkey carcass, with 2 cups cooked meat remaining on carcass
2 tablespoons canola oil
3 cups sweet onions, thinly sliced
1 teaspoon salt
1/2 teaspoon freshly ground black pepper
1/2 teaspoon ground sage
1/2 teaspoon dried thyme leaves
1-1/2 cups celery, cut into 1-inch pieces
2 cups carrots, peeled and sliced thin
2 cups green beans, cut into 1-inch pieces
2/3 cup small shell pasta

Remove meat from carcass and chop into bite size pieces. Cover and reserve in refrigerator. Chop turkey carcass into several large pieces. Heat oil in a large Dutch oven over medium heat. Sauté onions until soft and light brown. Stir in turkey bones, salt, pepper, herbs, and 2 quarts water. Increase heat to high and quickly bring mixture to a boil. Immediately reduce heat to low. Cover and simmer for one hour, stirring occasionally.

Remove and discard carcass pieces. Stir in vegetables; cover and continue to simmer for 20 to 25 minutes. Increase heat to high; bring mixture to a quick boil and stir in shell pasta. Lower heat to medium and cook 8 to 12 additional minutes until pasta and vegetables are tender. Stir in reserved turkey. Heat over low heat for 5 to 10 minutes or until the temperature reaches 165°. Serve hot with crusty rolls.

This recipe used by permission of the National Turkey Federation.

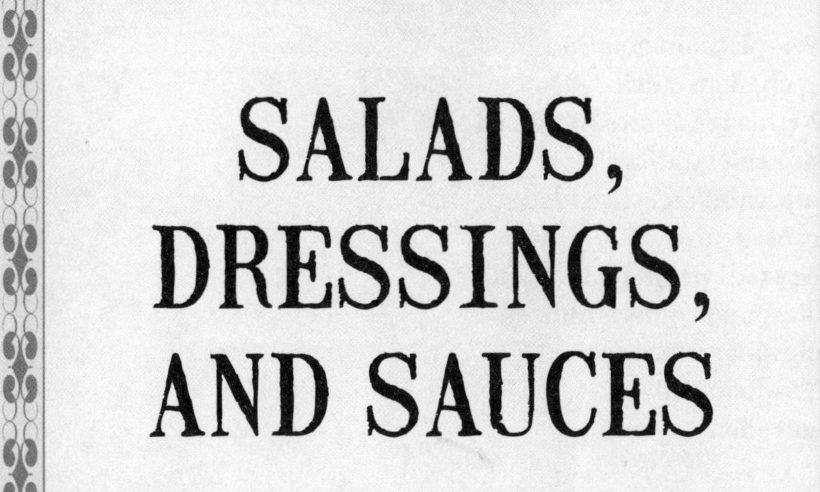

SALADS, DRESSINGS, AND SAUCES

Tomato Salad Cubes

1 envelope plain gelatin
1 cup chicken stock
1-1/2 cups fresh tomato, diced
1/2 cup celery, diced
1/2 cup cabbage, shredded
1 carrot, grated
1 green bell pepper, chopped
2 tablespoons onion, minced
2 tablespoons vinegar
1/2 teaspoon salt
1/4 teaspoon cayenne

Soak gelatin in stock; melt over hot water; add to other ingredients. Chill thoroughly in single ice tray with cube grid in position. Pile a few jellied cubes lightly on lettuce leaf; top with mayonnaise.

Frozen Nougat Cream Salad

1/2 teaspoon gelatin
1 tablespoon cold water
3 tablespoons cherry syrup
1/3 cup mayonnaise
1 cup cream, whipped
1/3 cup confectioner's sugar
1/4 teaspoon salt
6 marshmallows, diced
6 ounces maraschino cherries, minced
1/3 cup pecans, chopped

Soak gelatin in cold water; dissolve over hot water. Add to cherry syrup, then stir into mayonnaise. Fold whipped cream into mayonnaise mixture. Add remaining ingredients, freeze. Serve in squares in lettuce cups.

Frozen Fruit Salad

1 teaspoon gelatin
3 tablespoons syrup from canned fruit
1/2 cup mayonnaise
2/3 cup whipping cream
marshmallows, dates, and nuts, optional
2 cups canned fruit cocktail, drained
powdered sugar
salt
paprika

Soak gelatin in syrup and dissolve over hot water. Add slowly to mayonnaise. Beat cream and gradually beat into first mixture. Add marshmallows, dates, and nuts as desired. Add drained fruit and season to taste with sugar, salt, and paprika.

Molded Raw Cranberry Salad

2 cups water
1 envelope orange gelatin
juice of 1 lemon
2 cups raw cranberries, ground
1 cup celery, finely chopped

Pour 1/2 cup cold water in bowl. Add gelatin on top of water. Add 1-1/2 cups hot water and stir until dissolved. Add lemon juice. Set aside to cool. Add cranberries and celery to gelatin. Place salad in individual molds and let congeal in the refrigerator. Serve in lettuce cups.

Asparagus Bavarian Salad

1 tablespoon gelatin
1/4 cup cold water
1-1/2 cups asparagus liquid
1 can green asparagus
1/4 teaspoon salt
1/4 teaspoon white pepper
dash of mace
1/2 pimento, chopped
1 cup whipped evaporated milk

Soak gelatin in cold water. Open the can of asparagus, drain liquid, put vegetables aside, and heat the liquid. Pour into the gelatin and water mixture to dissolve. Chill. Arrange stalks of asparagus around the sides of a dampened salad mold. When the jelly begins to congeal, add 1/2 cup of asparagus that has been put through a sieve, salt, pepper, mace, the chopped pimento, and the whipped evaporated milk. Turn into the mold and set in the refrigerator to congeal. Serve with French dressing and mayonnaise. Garnish with pimento rings or strips.

Pineapple Carrot Salad Ring

1 cup water
1 package lemon gelatin
1 cup pineapple juice
4 or 5 carrots, grated
1 cup tidbits pineapple
lettuce
mayonnaise or French dressing

Heat 1 cup water and pour over gelatin. Add 1 cup cold pineapple juice. Simmer over low heat until gelatin is dissolved. Add grated carrot and pineapple. Place in in a large ring mold or individual molds. Place in refrigerator to congeal. Turn out on a bed of lettuce and garnish with French dressing or mayonnaise. If a large mold is used, the outside can be garnished with fruit, such as sliced pineapple, oranges, apricots, or pears.

Cheese Salad

1 package lemon-flavored gelatin
1 package lime-flavored gelatin
2 cups hot water
1 container creamed cottage cheese
1 can crushed pineapple
pinch of salt
1/2 cup pecans
lettuce
mayonnaise

Dissolve the gelatin in hot water; let cool. Add cheese and pineapple, blending well. Add salt and nuts. Chill several hours. Serve with lettuce and mayonnaise.

Shrimp Salad

3 cups shrimp, cooked
2 cups celery, diced
3 eggs, hard-boiled and diced
1/4 cup sweet pickles, chopped
2 tablespoons lemon juice
2 tablespoons pimento, minced
salt, to taste
mayonnaise
lettuce

Mix all ingredients, tossing lightly, and serve on bed of lettuce.

Golden Glow Salad

1 package orange gelatin
1 cup hot water
1 cup pineapple juice
1 tablespoon vinegar
1/2 teaspoon salt
1 cup canned pineapple, diced and drained
1 cup carrot, grated
lettuce
mayonnaise

Dissolve gelatin in hot water. Add pineapple juice, vinegar, and salt; chill. When slightly thickened add pineapple and carrot, chill until firm. Unmold on lettuce; garnish with mayonnaise.

Cabbage Salad

1 teaspoon sugar
1 teaspoon salt
1 egg
1/4 cup evaporated milk
1/4 cup water
1 tablespoon margarine
3 cups cabbage, finely chopped
1/2 cup hot vinegar

Mix sugar, salt, egg, milk, water, and margarine; stir over medium heat until thick. Stir in cabbage, toss with vinegar, and let cool.

Salmon Salad

1 (1-pound) can salmon, drained and broken into small pieces
1 cup celery, chopped
2 cups lettuce, torn into coarse threads
1/4 cup pickles, chopped
salt and pepper, to taste
French dressing
lettuce leaves
3 eggs, hardboiled and cut into wedges

Combine salmon, celery, lettuce, pickles, salt, and pepper; toss lightly. Dribble with French dressing and serve in cupped lettuce leaves. Garnish with egg wedges.

Hot Chicken Salad

2 cups chicken, cooked and cut into cubes
1-1/2 cups celery, diced
1/2 cup nuts, chopped
1 cup mayonnaise
2 tablespoons lemon juice
1/2 teaspoon salt
1/2 cup American or cheddar cheese, grated
1 cup potato chips, finely crushed

Combine chicken, celery, nuts, mayonnaise, lemon juice, and salt. Heat thoroughly. Pile into six small casseroles. Sprinkle with grated cheese, top with crushed potato chips. Bake at 400° for 10 minutes or until brown.

Easter Bunny Salad

6 pear halves
6 tablespoons cream cheese
6 lettuce leafs
12 almonds, blanched
12 whole cloves
6 teaspoons mayonnaise

Fill pears with cream cheese. Place on a lettuce leaf, round sides up. Stick cloves in each side of pear at the small end for eyes and the long almonds slightly behind the cloves for ears. Complete with a teaspoon of mayonnaise at the rough end for tail.

Green Pea Salad

1 large can green peas, drained
3 eggs, boiled and chopped
3/4 cup celery, chopped
1 large apple, chopped
2 sweet pickles, chopped
1 dill pickle, chopped
1 tablespoon pimento, chopped
2 tablespoons mayonnaise
salt and pepper, to taste
lettuce leaves

Mix all ingredients together and chill for two hours before serving. Serve on lettuce leaves with a dollop of mayonnaise.

Fruit Salad

3 apples
3 oranges
3 bananas
1 small can pineapple, drained
1 cup pecans
3 tablespoons mayonnaise

Peel apples, oranges, and bananas, and cut all ingredients into small pieces; mix with mayonnaise.

Pickle Chicken Salad

2 cups chicken, cooked and chopped
2 eggs, hard-boiled and chopped
1-1/2 cups celery, diced
1/2 cup sweet pickles, chopped
1/2 cup mayonnaise
1 teaspoon salt
1/8 teaspoon pepper

Combine chicken, eggs, celery, and pickles; mix well. Add mayonnaise, salt, and pepper. Mix together thoroughly and chill.

Seafood Salad

1/4 cup mayonnaise
1 tablespoon pickle juice
2 tablespoons sweet pickle, diced
1 cup canned tuna or shrimp
1/2 cup celery, sliced
1/2 cup canned peas, chilled
1 cup potato chips, coarsely crushed
lettuce

Mix mayonnaise with pickle juice. Combine with pickles, tuna or shrimp, celery, and peas. Toss, and add potato chips. Serve on lettuce.

Potato Salad

4 cups potatoes, cooked and diced
2 eggs, hard-boiled and chopped
1/2 cup celery, diced
1 teaspoon salt
1 dill pickle, chopped
1/2 teaspoon pepper
1/2 onion, finely chopped
1 tablespoon parsley, chopped
1 tablespoon pimento
mayonnaise
lettuce

Mix all ingredients except lettuce. Toss lightly with two forks to coat ingredients with mayonnaise. Serve on lettuce.

Macaroni Salad

2-1/2 cups elbow macaroni, cooked and drained
1 teaspoon salt
3 eggs, hard-boiled and sliced
1/3 cup sweet pickles, chopped
1 small can pimento, chopped
2 medium tomatoes, chopped
1 medium onion, chopped
1 carrot, chopped
2 celery sticks, chopped
1/2 cup mayonnaise
1 head lettuce

Combine all ingredients except lettuce. Mix well. Serve on salad dish lined with lettuce leaves.

Mixed Vegetable Salad

3 tomatoes, cut into wedges
1 green bell pepper, cut into rings
6 green onions, sliced
6 radishes, sliced
1 head lettuce, chopped
French dressing

Prepare and chill vegetables. Toss together with dressing.

Fresh Mushroom Sauce

1/3 cup butter
1 cup fresh mushrooms, sliced
1/4 cup flour
2-1/3 cups chicken broth
1/2 cup milk
1/2 teaspoon salt
dash of black pepper
1/4 teaspoon whole celery seed
fresh parsley, chopped

Sauté mushrooms in butter; blend in flour. Gradually stir in chicken broth and milk. Add seasoning and cook until medium thickness, stirring constantly. Garnish with parsley.

Seafood Cocktail Sauce

1/2 teaspoon horseradish sauce
12 drops hot sauce
1 tablespoon onion, minced
3 tablespoons lemon juice
2 tablespoons ketchup
dash salt

Mix all ingredients and chill. Serve with oysters, clams, crab, lobster, shrimp, or any fish.

Tartar Sauce

1 cup mayonnaise
1/2 cup sweet pickle relish
1/2 cup chopped onion

Mix all ingredients together. Store in refrigerator.

Barbecue Sauce

4 bottles ketchup
4 bottles steak sauce
1/4 cup garlic, minced
1 pint white vinegar
1-1/2 cups sugar
1 tablespoon salt

Mix all ingredients together. Store in refrigerator. Makes 1 gallon.

Cream or White Sauce

for a thin sauce:
1 tablespoon butter or margarine
1 tablespoon flour
1 cup milk
1/4 teaspoon salt

for a medium sauce:
2 tablespoons butter or margarine
2 tablespoons flour
1 cup milk
1/4 teaspoon salt

for a thick sauce:
3 tablespoons butter or margarine
3 tablespoons flour
1 cup milk
1 teaspoon salt

Melt the butter in a saucepan, then add flour, stirring until the mixture becomes foamy, but not brown. Gradually add milk; continue stirring to ensure smoothness; cook until thickened. Season. Each recipe makes about 1 cup.

Hollandaise Sauce

1/2 cup butter or margarine
2 egg yolks
1/4 teaspoon salt
dash of cayenne pepper
1 tablespoon lemon juice

Divide the butter into 3 pieces. Put 1 piece in a pan with the egg yolks and lemon juice and cook over hot water, stirring constantly with a wire whisk. Do not let the water touch the pan or the egg will cook too quickly. As the sauce thickens, add the second piece of butter, then the third. Remove from heat; add seasoning. One tablespoon of cream added helps to keep the sauce from separating. Good with eggs benedict and steamed asparagus or broccoli.

Tomato Sauce

2 cups canned tomatoes
1 teaspoon salt
2 tablespoons onion, chopped
1 bay leaf
3 to 4 peppercorns
1 to 2 celery stalks, chopped
2 tablespoons green bell pepper, chopped (optional)

Combine the ingredients and cook a few minutes to blend. Good with baked fish.

Golden Sauce

3 tablespoons butter or margarine
3 tablespoons flour
1-1/2 cups milk
1/4 teaspoon salt
1/8 teaspoon pepper
2 egg yolks
1 teaspoon lemon juice

Melt the butter; add the flour and milk slowly, stirring constantly. Season. Beat the egg yolks. Add a small amount of sauce slowly to the egg yolks, then combine with the rest of the sauce. After the eggs have been added, do not place over direct heat. Just before serving, add lemon juice.

Mint Sauce

8 stalks mint, or 2 tablespoons dry mint
2 tablespoons sugar
1/2 cup vinegar

Wash the mint and pick the leaves from the stems. Chop fine. Add sugar to the vinegar. Pour over the mint leaves. Let stand 1 hour. Good over salmon, roast lamb, or steamed vegetables.

Mayonnaise

1/2 teaspoon dry mustard
1 teaspoon salt
dash of pepper
1 teaspoon sugar
1 egg yolk*
2 tablespoons vinegar or lemon juice, or both
1 cup salad oil

Combine the dry ingredients and the egg yolk. Mix well and stir in 1/2 teaspoon of vinegar or lemon juice. Add oil, drop by drop at first, beating with a rotary egg beater or hand mixer. As oil and other ingredients blend, more oil may be added at a time. As the mixture begins to thicken, add the remaining vinegar or lemon juice. Continue to beat until the dressing is very stiff. It may be stored in a covered jar in the refrigerator.

*See page 178 for information about cooking with raw eggs.

Boiled Salad Dressing

1 teaspoon salt
1 teaspoon dry mustard
2 teaspoons sugar
pinch of cayenne
2-1/2 tablespoons flour
2 egg yolks, or 1 egg
2 tablespoons melted butter or margarine
3/4 cup milk
1/2 cup vinegar

Mix the dry ingredients and add the egg yolks (slightly beaten), butter or margarine, milk, and vinegar, slowly. Cook in a double boiler until the mixture thickens. Cool before using. If cooked too long it will curdle.

French Dressing

1 teaspoon salt
1/2 teaspoon dry mustard
1/2 teaspoon paprika
1/2 teaspoon sugar
1 cup salad oil
1/3 cup vinegar

Mix the dry ingredients in a bowl. Add salad oil and blend well. Add vinegar and beat until thickened slightly. French dressing may be made in quantity and kept covered in refrigerator. It should be well shaken before using.

Thousand Island Dressing

1 cup mayonnaise
4 tablespoons chili sauce
1/2 teaspoon Worcestershire sauce
1 egg, hard-boiled and finely chopped

Place all ingredients except egg in a mixing bowl and beat until well blended. Fold in egg with a spoon.

Sour Cream Dressing

3 tablespoons vinegar
1 cup evaporated milk, undiluted
1/2 teaspoon salt

Add the vinegar slowly to milk and beat until smooth. Add salt. Excellent to serve on chopped raw cabbage and with other vegetable salads.

Mama Doris's Homestyle Gravy

1/2 cup meat drippings
3/4 cup all-purpose flour
1 teaspoon salt
1 teaspoon pepper
4 cups water or milk

Heat the meat drippings in a skillet over medium heat. Whisk in the flour, salt, and pepper; continue whisking until smooth. Slowly stir in the milk and continue cooking until thickened.

BREADS

Foundation Refrigerator Dough (3 in 1)

4 eggs, beaten well
1/2 pound butter, melted
3/4 cup sugar
2 cups sour cream
1 teaspoon salt
2 compressed yeast cakes
3 tablespoons warm milk
6 cups flour

Combine beaten eggs, melted butter, sugar, sour cream, and salt in large bowl. Add yeast (dissolved in warm milk); add flour, sifted once after measuring. Mix thoroughly with wooden spoon. Shape like any dough. Chill overnight in refrigerator in covered greased bowl.

To make rolls, pinch off needed quantity; shape, let rise in pans about 20 minutes before baking. Bake at 400° for 20 minutes.

To make tea cakes, roll dough 1/4-inch thick; cut plain or fancy; dust with sugar, spices and nuts; let rise 20 minutes; bake at 400° for 20 minutes .

Plain Muffins

2 cups flour
1 tablespoon baking powder
1/2 teaspoon salt
1 tablespoon sugar
1 cup milk
1 egg
2 tablespoons shortening, melted

Mix and sift the dry ingredients. Combine the milk and well-beaten egg. Add gradually to the dry ingredients, stirring well. Add melted shortening. Grease the muffin tins; fill them two-thirds full. Bake about 25 minutes at 425°. Makes a dozen medium-sized muffins.

Bran Muffins

2 tablespoons shortening
1/4 cup sugar
1 egg
1 cup bran
3/4 cup milk
1 cup flour
2-1/2 teaspoons baking powder
1/2 teaspoon salt

Cream the shortening and sugar. Add the egg and beat well. Add the bran and milk. Let soak until most of the moisture disappears. Stir in the sifted dry ingredients. Grease the muffin tins; fill two-thirds full. Bake at 400° for about 30 minutes. Makes 8 large muffins.

Mama Doris's Famous Biscuits

2 cups flour
3 teaspoons baking powder
1/2 teaspoon salt
1/4 cup shortening
3/4 cup milk

Mix and sift the dry ingredients. Blend in the shortening with a pastry blender or the tips of the fingers. The mixture should resemble coarse cornmeal. Add the milk, stirring with a fork. Turn out onto a slightly floured board. Knead lightly for about 30 seconds and roll to 1/2-inch thickness. Cut with a floured biscuit cutter. Bake on an ungreased sheet at 400° from 12 to 15 minutes. Makes 14 to 16 biscuits.

Popovers

1 cup flour
1/4 teaspoon salt
1 cup milk
2 eggs

Sift the flour and salt into a bowl. Combine the milk and well-beaten eggs and stir gradually into the dry ingredients to make a smooth batter. Beat for about 2 minutes. Fill hot greased muffin pans two-thirds full. Bake at 450° about 35 minutes until they pop. Reduce the heat to 350° and bake 15 minutes longer. Serve immediately. Makes 8 popovers.

Cornbread

1 cup cornmeal
1/4 cup flour
1-1/2 teaspoons baking powder
1/2 teaspoon salt
2 eggs
1/2 cup milk
1/4 cup shortening, melted

Mix and sift the dry ingredients. Combine the eggs and milk and stir into the dry ingredients. Stir in melted shortening and pour into a greased baking pan. Bake at 425° for about 25 minutes. Makes 12 servings.

Peanut Butter Bread

2 cups flour
4 teaspoons baking powder
1 teaspoon salt
1/3 cup sugar
1/2 cup peanut butter
3/4 cup evaporated milk mixed with 3/4 cup water

Mix and sift the dry ingredients. Add the peanut butter and cut in well with pastry blender or two knives. Add the milk and beat thoroughly. Pour into a greased loaf-cake pan and bake at 350° for about 1 hour.

Boston Brown Bread

1 cup cornmeal
1 cup rye flour
1 cup graham flour
1 teaspoon salt
2-1/4 teaspoons baking soda
2 cups sour milk
3/4 cup molasses
1/2 cup raisins, if desired

Mix together the dry ingredients. Combine well with the sour milk and molasses. If the mixture is too stiff, thin it with a little water. If raisins are used, either add them to the dry mixture before the liquid is added, or reserve a little flour, sift well over the raisins, and stir in last. Fill well-greased molds two-thirds full and tie the lids, which also must be greased. Steam 3 hours or more, depending on the size of the molds used.

Keep the water boiling and the kettle covered all the time during the steaming. Add more boiling water, if necessary. Remove the molds from the water; uncover. Bake at 250° to dry for about 30 minutes.

Gingerbread

2 cups flour
3/4 teaspoon baking soda
1/2 teaspoon salt
2 teaspoons ginger
1 teaspoon cinnamon
1/2 cup evaporated milk
1/2 cup water
1 tablespoon vinegar
1 cup molasses
1/4 cup shortening, melted

Mix and sift the dry ingredients. Add remaining ingredients and stir until smooth. Pour into a greased 9-inch layer-cake pan. Bake at 350° for 30 minutes.

Date Oatmeal Loaf

1 cup quick-cooking rolled oats
1 cup chopped dates
1-1/4 cups scalding milk
1 egg, slightly beaten
3/4 cup light corn syrup
2 cups flour
4 teaspoons baking powder
1 teaspoon salt

Add rolled oats and dates to the milk; let stand for 10 minutes. Add the egg and corn syrup. Mix and sift the dry ingredients. Add the milk mixture, stirring only enough to blend well. Bake in a greased loaf pan at 350° for 1 hour.

Plain Bread

2 cups milk
1/4 cup light corn syrup or honey
4 teaspoons salt
2 tablespoons shortening
2 cups water
1 cake yeast, compressed or dry granular
1/4 cup lukewarm water
12 cups flour

Scald the milk. Add the syrup or honey, salt, shortening, and water. Cool until it is lukewarm. Add the yeast that has been softened in 1/4 cup of lukewarm water. Add the flour gradually, mixing it in thoroughly. When the dough is stiff, turn out on a lightly floured board and knead until it is smooth and satiny. Shape into a smooth ball. Place in a greased bowl. Cover and let it rise in a warm place (80° to 85°) until doubled in bulk. This will require about 4 or 5 hours. Punch down. Let it rise again. When it is light, divide it into four equal portions. Round up each portion into a smooth ball. Cover well and let it rest from 10 to 15 minutes. Mold into loaves. Place in greased bread pans. Let it rise until doubled in bulk. Bake at 400° from 40 to 45 minutes. Makes 4 one-pound loaves.

Refrigerator Rolls

2 cakes yeast, compressed or dry granular
1/4 cup lukewarm water
1 cup milk
1/2 cup light corn syrup, or 1/4 cup honey
1 tablespoon salt
6 cups flour
2 eggs
1/2 cup shortening, melted

Soften the yeast in lukewarm water. Scald the milk, and add the syrup and salt. Add 2 cups of flour and beat well. Add the yeast. Beat the eggs and add them. Blend well. Add the shortening. Add the remaining flour to make a soft dough. Knead until smooth and satiny. Place in a lightly greased bowl; grease the top of the dough. Cover well and put it into the refrigerator. When wanted, remove the dough from the refrigerator and punch down. Mold at once in any desired shape. Or, if preferred, let the dough stand in a warm room for an hour before molding. Place the rolls in greased pans, cover, and let them rise until doubled in bulk. Bake at 425° for 15 to 20 minutes. Makes about 2-1/2 dozen rolls.

Banana Bread

1 cup sugar
1/2 cup shortening
2 eggs
2 large bananas, mashed
2 cups flour
1/2 cup nuts
1 teaspoon baking soda
1 teaspoon salt

Cream together sugar and shortening. Add remaining ingredients. Pour batter into a well-greased loaf pan and bake at 350° for 1 hour or until done.

Cracklin' Bread

1-1/2 cups cornmeal
3/4 cup flour
1/2 teaspoon baking soda
1/4 teaspoon salt
1 cup sour milk
1 cup cracklings, diced

Mix and sift together the dry ingredients. Add the milk. Stir in cracklings. Form into small oblong cakes and place in a greased baking pan. Bake at 400° for 30 minutes.

Whole Wheat Bread

1/2 cup dark brown sugar
1/2 cup dark molasses
1 egg
3/4 teaspoon soda
2 tablespoons hot water
1 cup milk
2 teaspoons baking powder
1 teaspoon salt
3 cups whole wheat flour
1 cup nuts
1 cup raisins

In a large bowl combine brown sugar and molasses. Add egg and baking soda that's been dissolved in hot water. Stir well. As you stir, gradually add milk. Sift baking powder with salt and flour. Reserve 2 tablespoons. Add the rest to the batter a bit at a time, stirring well after each addition. Dredge nuts and raisins in reserved flour mixture and add to batter. Pour into a well-greased baking pan and bake at 350° for about 1 hour.

Sweet Milk Griddlecakes

3 cups flour
3/4 teaspoon salt
6 teaspoons baking powder
1 tablespoon sugar
1 egg
2 cups milk
2 tablespoons shortening, melted

Combine all the dry ingredients and sift. Beat the eggs and milk. Add to the sifted dry ingredients and beat thoroughly. Stir in melted shortening. Place the batter in a pitcher. Pour on a hot griddle. Bake on one side, turn, and bake on the other side. If thinner batter is preferred, use more milk.

Cornmeal Griddlecakes

1 cup flour
4 teaspoons baking powder
1 teaspoon salt
1 cup cornmeal
1 egg, well beaten
2 cups milk
2 tablespoons shortening, melted

Sift the flour, baking powder, and salt together. Add the cornmeal and mix well. Combine the beaten egg and milk and add to the dry ingredients. Stir in the shortening. Bake the same way as other griddlecakes.

Hush Puppies

1 egg
3/4 cup buttermilk
3/4 cup flour
1-1/2 cups cornmeal
2 teaspoons baking powder
1/2 teaspoon salt
1/2 teaspoon baking soda
1/2 cup onion, chopped

Mix egg and milk together. Sift dry ingredients together and add to milk mixture. Stir lightly. Add onion. Drop balls of dough into hot oil. Fry until golden brown. Makes about 2 dozen.

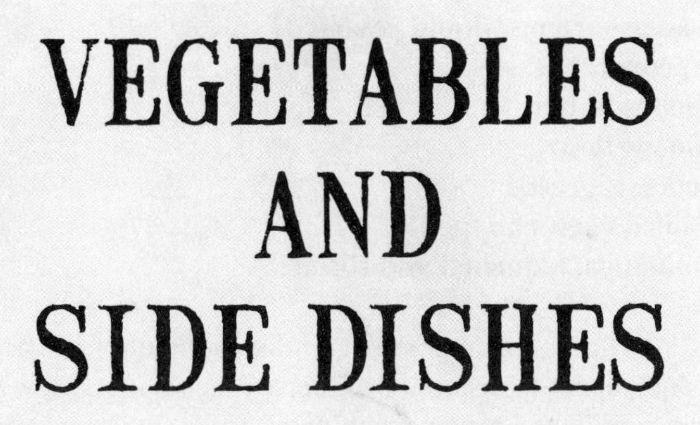

VEGETABLES AND SIDE DISHES

Asparagus Casserole

2 cups scalded milk
1 large can asparagus, liquid reserved
salt and pepper, to taste
2 tablespoons butter
2 tablespoons flour
1/2 cup cheese, grated
3 hard-boiled eggs, chopped
1/2 cup almonds, blanched and sliced

In a small bowl, mix together scalded milk and liquid from asparagus. Add salt and pepper to taste. In a saucepan, melt butter. Slowly add flour; pour in milk and asparagus mixture. Cook until thick and smooth but do not boil. Add grated cheese and keep hot until melted.

Place alternate layers of asparagus, hard-boiled eggs, almonds, and sauce in a casserole. Season as desired. Bake at 350° until lightly browned.

Cabbage Rolls

1/2 pound ground beef
1/2 cup 1-minute rice, uncooked
1/2 cup onions, finely chopped
1/2 teaspoon chili powder
salt and pepper, to taste
cabbage leaves
1 (14-ounce) can tomatoes

Mix all ingredients, except cabbage leaves and tomatoes. Roll in cabbage leaves and place in a pressure cooker, pour tomatoes on top of rolls. Cook 7 to 8 minutes at 10 pounds pressure.

Macaroni and Cheese

1 (8-ounce) package macaroni
4 tablespoons butter or fortified margarine
1/4 cup flour
1 teaspoon salt
1/4 teaspoon pepper
2 cups milk
1/4 pound cheese, cut in small pieces

Cook the macaroni as directed on the package. Melt the butter, add the flour, season, and blend. Add the milk slowly and cook at low temperature until thick and smooth. Add the cheese and stir until the cheese has melted. Place the macaroni in a greased 2-quart baking dish. Pour cheese sauce over it. Bake at 375° for 25 to 30 minutes. Makes 6 servings.

Macaroni with Tomato Sauce

1 (8-ounce) package macaroni, spaghetti, or noodles
2 cups canned tomatoes or tomato juice
1/4 cup green bell pepper, chopped
1 onion, sliced
1/2 teaspoon salt
1/8 teaspoon pepper
1/4 pound cheese

Cook and drain the macaroni according to the directions on the package. Make a sauce by cooking together tomatoes, pepper, sliced onion, and seasonings. Place the macaroni in a greased casserole. Pour the sauce over it. Dot the top with cheese cut into pieces. Bake at 350° for 25 to 30 minutes.

Spanish Rice

3 tablespoons vegetable oil
1 medium-sized onion, minced
1/4 cup green bell pepper, chopped
1 garlic clove, minced
2-1/2 cups canned tomatoes or tomato juice
1 teaspoon salt
3 cups rice, cooked

Heat the vegetable oil in a frying pan. Add the onion, pepper, and garlic, and cook 2 or 3 minutes. Add the tomatoes and salt and blend well. Stir in the rice. Cover the pan and cook at low temperature until the tomato juice is absorbed, about 15 minutes. Makes 6 servings.

Baked Beans

3 cups dried beans
1/4 pound salt pork
2 tablespoons molasses
2 tablespoons sugar
1/4 teaspoon mustard
2 teaspoons salt

Pick over the beans and wash them thoroughly. Soak them overnight in cold water. Add enough cold water to cover and cook slowly for 45 minutes. Pour the beans into a baking dish. Cut the pork into 1/2-inch strips; bury in beans. Mix the molasses, sugar, mustard, and salt with enough boiling water to dissolve. Pour the mixture over the beans, adding enough boiling water to cover. Cover the pan and bake at 325° from 4 to 6 hours.

Scalloped Cabbage with Cheese and Tomatoes

4 cups cooked cabbage
1 cup canned tomatoes
salt and pepper, to taste
1/4 pound cheese, grated
2 cups bread crumbs
2 tablespoons butter or margarine

In a greased casserole, place layers of cabbage and tomatoes, season and sprinkle with cheese and bread crumbs. Dot the top layer of bread crumbs with butter. Bake at 350° for 30 minutes, or heat thoroughly over hot water until the cheese is melted.

Savory Red Cabbage

4 cups shredded red cabbage
1/4 cup vinegar
3/4 cup water
1/4 cup brown sugar
1/4 teaspoon ground cloves, or 5 whole ones
2 tart apples, diced
1 teaspoon salt

Combine all the ingredients and cook at low temperature until the cabbage and apples are tender, or for about 20 minutes.

Stuffed Eggplant

1 eggplant
2 tablespoons minced onion
2 tablespoons butter
1 cup fresh tomatoes, chopped
1 cup soft bread crumbs
1 teaspoon salt

Wash the eggplant and cut in half. Scoop out the pulp to 1/2-inch of the skin. Dice the pulp. Brown the onion in the butter, add the eggplant pulp, tomatoes, bread crumbs, and salt. Mix well and fill the eggplant shells with the mixture. Bake at 375° until browned, or about 30 minutes.

Okra, Rice, and Tomatoes

1 cup rice
2 tablespoons butter or margarine
salt and pepper
dash of paprika
1 quart okra
1/2 can tomatoes
1 onion, sliced

Wash the rice and cook in boiling salted water until tender. Drain and add butter, salt, pepper, and paprika. Cut the okra in slices and cook in a small quantity of boiling water. When nearly done, add the tomatoes, onion, and rice. Serve hot.

Scalloped Tomatoes

1 can tomatoes
1 teaspoon salt
dash of pepper
2 cups bread crumbs
2 tablespoons butter or margarine

Season tomatoes with salt and pepper. A suggestion of minced onion and green pepper may be added also. Fill a baking dish or casserole with bread crumbs and tomatoes in alternate layers, having the bread crumbs on top. Dot with butter or margarine. Bake at 350° about 1/2 hour.

Vegetable Noodle Bake

1 pound green string beans cut in 1-1/2-inch pieces
2 cups carrots, diced
4 cups medium white sauce (see page 31)
3 ounces broad noodles
1 teaspoon salt
pepper
1/2 teaspoon Worcestershire sauce
1 cup grated American cheese
2 cups soft bread crumbs, buttered

Cook the beans and carrots in boiling salted water. Drain and combine any leftover cooking water with milk in making white sauce. Cook the noodles according to the directions on the package. Add seasonings and cheese to white sauce. Combine with the vegetables and noodles. Pour into a greased shallow baking dish. Cover with buttered crumbs. Bake at 350° from 20 to 25 minutes, or until browned. Makes 6 to 8 servings.

Alabama Green Beans

2 slices bacon
1 small onion, grated
1/4 cup ketchup
1 teaspoon Worcestershire sauce
salt and pepper, to taste
1-1/2 pounds green beans, cooked

In a skillet, cook the bacon. Remove bacon and discard drippings except for 2 tablespoons left in skillet. Brown the onions in the bacon drippings, then stir in seasonings. Pour mixture over the green beans. Heat thoroughly and serve.

Scalloped Potatoes

1/2 cup onion, minced
6 tablespoons butter
6 tablespoons flour
1-1/2 teaspoons salt
1/2 teaspoon pepper
3 cups milk
4 cups Irish potatoes, sliced and cooked
1/2 pound cheddar cheese, sliced

In a saucepan, cook onions in butter over low heat; add flour, salt, and pepper and stir until blended. Remove from heat gradually. Stir in milk and return to heat, stirring constantly until thick and smooth. Remove from heat and set aside. In a shallow baking dish arrange layers of the potatoes, onion sauce, and the cheese. Bake at 350° until cheese melts and browns. Makes 8 servings.

Sweet and Sour Cabbage

1 head of cabbage
2 cups boiling water
4 slices of bacon, diced
2 tablespoons brown sugar
2 tablespoons flour
1/2 cup water
1/3 cup vinegar
salt and pepper, to taste
1 small onion, sliced

Cook cabbage in boiling water for 7 minutes. Drain. Fry bacon in a pan and remove. Add brown sugar and flour to bacon drippings; blend well. Add water, vinegar, and seasonings. Cook until thick, about 5 minutes; add onion, cooked bacon, and cabbage. Heat thoroughly. Makes 4 servings.

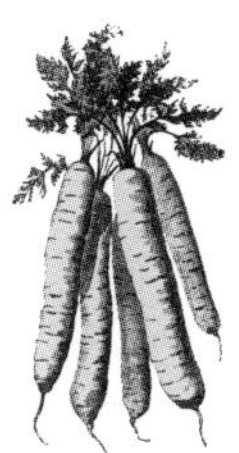

Stuffed Squash

6 medium squash
1 teaspoon celery, minced
1 teaspoon onion, minced
1 teaspoon green bell pepper, minced
2 tablespoons bacon grease
2 tablespoons butter
1 cup bread crumbs
1 egg
1/2 cup milk
salt and pepper, to taste

Boil squash in salted water until tender. Split in half. Scoop out middle, remove large seeds, and mash the pulp. Save shells to stuff. Slowly sauté celery, onion, and bell pepper in bacon grease. Do not brown. Mix with mashed squash. Beat in egg and add milk. Season to taste. Melt butter and pour over bread crumbs. Mix 3/4 cup of the bread crumbs into squash mixture and fill shells. Sprinkle the remaining bread crumbs over tops of squash and bake at 400° for 15 minutes or until brown.

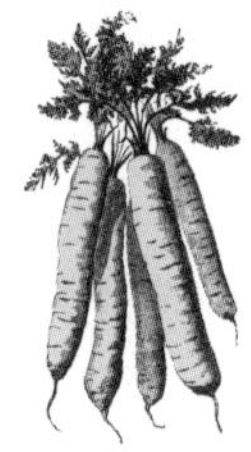

Creamy Spinach

1 (12-ounce) package frozen spinach
1 tablespoon butter
1 teaspoon onion, finely minced
1 tablespoon flour
dash of nutmeg, salt, and pepper
1 cup milk
1 tablespoon heavy cream

Boil spinach in a small amount of water until tender. Drain and chop. Then add butter and onion; simmer for 1 minute. Sprinkle with flour and add nutmeg, salt, and pepper, stirring well. Add milk and heat, but do not boil. Just before serving stir in heavy cream.

Stuffed Bell Peppers

6 bell peppers
1 cup ground beef
1 medium onion
1 cup tomatoes
1/2 cup rice, cooked
salt and pepper, to taste
1/2 cup flour

Boil peppers for 10 minutes. Drain, cool, and cut into halves. Set aside. In a saucepan, brown the beef and the onion. Drain. Add tomatoes, rice, and seasoning, and cook for 5 more minutes. Slowly stir in the flour and continue stirring until the mixture thickens. Remove from heat. Fill each pepper with mixture and bake at 350° for 25 minutes.

Onion Rings

2 cups flour, divided
1/4 cup baking powder
1/2 teaspoon salt
1-1/4 cups milk
3 large onions, sliced and separated into rings
vegetable oil

Sift 1-1/2 cups flour, baking powder, and salt together and add to milk. Dip each onion ring in batter until well coated but not dripping. Dredge in remaining flour. Fill a deep pot with 1-inch of vegetable oil and heat. Fry onion rings in hot oil until golden brown.

Okra and Tomatoes

3 tablespoons butter
2 medium onions, sliced
3 medium tomatoes
salt and pepper, to taste
2-1/2 cups okra, sliced
1 teaspoon sugar

Melt butter in a skillet; add the sliced onions and tomatoes. Sprinkle with salt and pepper. Cover and simmer 3 minutes. Slide okra slices over top of tomatoes to preserve color. Sprinkle with salt, pepper, and sugar. Cover and continue to simmer until okra is tender, about 5 minutes. Season to taste. Makes 5 servings.

Potato Pancakes

3 large potatoes, grated and squeezed dry
3 tablespoons flour
1 teaspoon sugar
1 medium onion, grated
2 teaspoons baking powder
1-1/2 teaspoons parsley, chopped
1 egg, beaten
1/8 teaspoon pepper
1 teaspoon salt

Mix all ingredients together thoroughly. Drop by tablespoons into hot oil. Fry until golden brown. Drain.

Cabbage Slaw

1 medium head cabbage
4 large carrots
1 medium onion
1 teaspoon salt
1/2 teaspoon celery salt
3 tablespoons sugar
2 cups vinegar, hot
mayonnaise

Finely chop all of the vegetables; add salt, celery salt, sugar, and hot vinegar. Let stand for one hour. Drain thoroughly and add mayonnaise. Chill.

Cheese Soufflé

3 tablespoons butter or fortified margarine
3 tablespoons flour
1 cup milk
1/2 teaspoon salt
1/8 teaspoon pepper
1 cup cheese, cut in small pieces
3 eggs, separated

Melt the butter, add flour and milk gradually. Cook at low temperature until thick and smooth. Remove from the heat; add seasonings and cheese, stirring occasionally to blend the cheese with the sauce. When slightly cooled, add beaten egg yolks and fold in stiffly beaten egg whites. Pour into an ungreased casserole or deep baking dish. Bake at 350° until nicely browned on top, about 45 to 50 minutes. Serve immediately.

Creamed Eggs and Potatoes

2 tablespoons butter or margarine
2 tablespoons flour
salt
1 cup evaporated milk
1 cup water
4 large potatoes (boiled in skins)
4 hard-cooked eggs, sliced

Melt the butter, add flour, salt, and evaporated milk mixed with water, and cook until slightly thickened. Add potatoes diced and eggs. Reheat.

Pepper and Tomato Relish

8 ripe tomatoes, peeled and quartered
6 small onions, chopped
3 small green bell peppers, chopped
1 cup brown sugar
1 cup vinegar
1-1/2 tablespoons salt
1/4 teaspoon allspice
1/2 tablespoon cinnamon
1/4 tablespoon cloves

Combine the tomatoes, onions, and bell peppers. Add the sugar, vinegar, salt, and spices tied in cheesecloth. Cook slowly in a heavy kettle for about 2 hours, stirring frequently. Remove the spice bag and pour the mixture into sterilized jars. Seal immediately.

Tomato Jelly

1 tablespoon gelatin
1/4 cup cold water
2 cups tomato juice
1 small onion, sliced
1 bay leaf
3 peppercorns
celery tops
2 tablespoons lemon juice or vinegar

Soften gelatin in cold water. Cook tomato juice and other ingredients for about 10 minutes. Strain and add to the gelatin. Pour into individual molds and chill until firm. Remove from mold and serve with any greens. Use any desired dressing. This quantity will fill from 5 to 6 small individual molds.

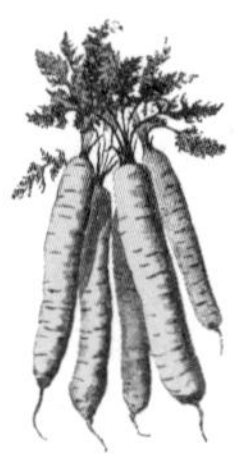

BEEF, PORK, AND LAMB

Ground Beef and Potatoes

1 pound ground beef
8 medium Irish potatoes
1 cup hot water
1 teaspoon salt
1/2 teaspoon pepper
1 tablespoon flour
1 cup milk

Brown and drain ground beef. Stir slowly until brown. Cut potatoes into six pieces each and add them to the beef. Add hot water, salt, and pepper and cook slowly, covered. Make a paste of flour and milk. Add the paste and simmer until thick. Remove from heat. Keep covered until ready to serve. Serves about 8.

Baked Beef Hash

2 tablespoons onion, diced
2 tablespoons green bell pepper, diced
1 tablespoon margarine
2 cups beef, cooked and shredded
1 (10-ounce) can condensed beef soup with vegetables, undiluted
1 cup potatoes, cooked and diced
1 egg

Sauté onions and green pepper in margarine until tender. Add beef, soup, and potatoes. Simmer for 5 minutes, stirring occasionally. Remove from stove top; add egg and mix thoroughly. Place in a greased casserole and bake at 400° for 45 minutes. Cut into squares for serving. Makes 6 servings.

Meatloaf

1 pound ground meat
1 egg, well beaten
1/4 cup ketchup (optional)
1 teaspoon salt
1/4 teaspoon pepper
2 tablespoons onion, chopped
1 teaspoon Worcestershire sauce
2/3 cup water
2/3 cup oatmeal

Ground beef, veal, or lamb, or a combination of the three, may be used. Combine the ingredients in the order given. Mix well. Pack in a greased loaf-pan. Bake at 375° for 1 hour. May be served hot or cold.

Meatloaf №2

1-1/2 pounds hamburger meat
1 cup corn bread crumbs
1 cup sweet milk
1 egg
salt, to taste

Mix all ingredients and put into a loaf pan. Bake at 375° for 1-1/2 hours.

Spaghetti and Beef Dinner

1 pound ground beef
1 small onion, chopped
1 teaspoon Worcestershire sauce
1 cup tomato juice
1/2 pound spaghetti
1/4 pound cheese, shredded

Put all ingredients, except spaghetti and cheese, into a frying pan. Cook until beef is done. While cooking, prepare spaghetti according to instructions on package. When spaghetti is done, add it to the frying pan. Mix thoroughly. Pour into a baking dish, top with cheese, and bake for 20 minutes at 450°.

Hamburger Beans

1 pound hamburger meat
1 tablespoon onion, grated
1 small garlic clove
2 cups dried beans, cooked
1/2 cup ketchup
1 cup tomato soup
salt, to taste

Brown the meat, onion, and garlic. Pour off excess grease then add the beans, ketchup, and tomato soup. Let simmer slowly for about 30 minutes. Season to taste. Serve hot with toast.

Steak Stroganoff

1 pound round steak, cubed
1/4 cup flour
1 tablespoon oil
1/2 cup onions, chopped
1 garlic clove, minced
1 (6-ounce) can mushrooms and broth
1 cup sour cream
1 can mushroom soup
1 tablespoon Worcestershire sauce
1/2 teaspoon salt
1/8 teaspoon pepper
2 cups hot cooked rice

Roll meat in flour, then brown in hot oil in a large frying pan. Remove meat; add onion, garlic, and mushrooms. Cook gently until onions are golden. Add remaining ingredients except rice. Cook until thickened. Return meat to the pan and simmer, stirring occasionally, about 1 hour or until meat is tender. Serve over fluffy cooked rice.

Veal Cutlets

2-1/2 pounds veal (from round)
salt and pepper
1 egg
1 tablespoon water
fine bread crumbs
6 tablespoons butter or margarine
2 tablespoons flour
2 cups stock, water, or strained tomatoes or tomato juice
1 teaspoon Worcestershire sauce
2 tablespoons parsley, chopped

Wipe the meat and cut it into pieces for individual serving, removing the bone, skin, and tough membranes. Season with salt and pepper. Beat the egg and water. Dip the meat in sifted seasoned bread crumbs; dip in egg, then in crumbs again. Melt 4 tablespoons of butter in a frying pan. When hot, brown the cutlets quickly on both sides.

Melt remaining 2 tablespoons butter in a saucepan, then add flour, stirring until the mixture becomes foamy, but not brown. Add stock; continue stirring to insure smoothness; cook until thickened. Season to taste with Worcestershire sauce, parsley, salt, and pepper.

Pour the sauce over the cutlets, cover, then cook at a low temperature for 1 hour or until tender, turning occasionally.

Flank or Round Steak, Stuffed and Rolled

1 onion, sliced
4 tablespoons melted butter or margarine, divided
2 cups bread crumbs
poultry seasoning
1/2 teaspoon salt
pepper
1 cup boiling water or stock
1 pound flank or round steak, 1/2-inch thick
1/4 cup carrot, cubed

Brown the onion in 2 tablespoons melted butter; add the bread crumbs, seasoning, and water or stock. Spread over the meat. Roll, and tie securely. Brown in remaining butter in a heavy pot. Add water or stock and carrot. Simmer gently on top of the stove for 1-1/2 hours or bake at 350° for the same length of time.

Creamed Liver

1 pound liver
2 tablespoons butter or margarine
2 tablespoons flour
3/4 teaspoon salt
1-1/2 cups milk
1 tablespoon green bell pepper, chopped
1 teaspoon onion, minced

Drop the liver in salted, boiling water and cook for 5 to 10 minutes; then dice. Melt the butter, add the flour, seasoning, and milk. Stir until smooth; add diced liver, onion, and green pepper. May be served on toast.

Liver Loaf

1 pound liver
1 onion
1 cup bread crumbs
1 egg, slightly beaten
1 cup milk
1 teaspoon salt

Drop the liver in salted boiling water and cook for 5 to 10 minutes. Grind in a food processor together with the onion; add crumbs, egg, milk, and salt; mix well and put in a greased baking dish. Set in a pan of hot water and bake for 1/2 hour at 350°.

Liver with Vegetables

6 small onions, chopped
2 tablespoons flour
1 pound liver, sliced
1 tablespoon butter
2 cups water
1 cup peas
1 cup canned tomatoes
2 carrots, diced
2 turnips, diced
salt and pepper, to taste

Brown 1 onion, flour, and liver in butter. Cut the liver into small pieces. Add water, peas, tomatoes, carrots, turnips, seasoning, and the remaining onions. Cook for about 20 minutes until the vegetables are done.

Liver with Rice or Potatoes

1 pound liver
2 cups canned tomatoes
1 medium onion
3 cups cooked rice or potatoes
salt, to taste

Drop the liver in boiling salted water and cook for 5 to 10 minutes. Remove from the water and cut into small pieces. Combine with tomatoes, onion, rice, or potatoes. Season to taste. Cook a few minutes until the flavor is blended.

Liver-stuffed Green Peppers

1/2 pound liver
6 green peppers
1 cup cooked rice
1/2 cup canned tomatoes
1-1/2 tablespoons onion, minced
1 teaspoon salt
1 cup hot water

Drop the liver in boiling salted water and cook from 5 to 10 minutes. Grind in a meat chopper. Remove the seeds from peppers. Parboil for a few minutes in boiling salted water. Mix all the ingredients except water and stuff the peppers. Set in baking dish, pour hot water around the peppers, and bake for 30 minutes at 350°.

Shepherd's Pie

2 cups meat, cooked and chopped
2 cups leftover gravy
1 tablespoon onion, finely chopped
1 teaspoon salt
1/8 teaspoon pepper
1/8 teaspoon paprika
2 cups mashed potatoes
2 tablespoons butter or margarine

Combine meat, gravy, onion, and seasonings. Line the bottom of a buttered baking dish with well-beaten mashed potato. Or, meat and gravy may be placed in the lower part of the baking dish with a single thick layer of mashed potato for the crust. Dot with bits of butter or margarine. Bake at 400° until the potatoes are brown, or if cold potatoes have been used, until thoroughly heated and browned. Crumbs, macaroni, or rice may be substituted for potatoes.

Hash

1 to 2 cups meat
2 cups cooked potato
1 teaspoon onion, minced
enough milk, water, or stock to moisten
1 teaspoon salt
1/4 teaspoon pepper
3 to 4 tablespoons butter or margarine

Chop the meat first, then add the potato and chop together. Add onion. Moisten it enough to hold together. Season. Melt the butter (1 tablespoon to each cup of hash) in a frying pan, spread the hash in evenly, and cook slowly from 20 to 30 minutes. When the hash is well browned, loosen it with a spatula, and turn one half of it over the other half.

Baked Rice and Meat

2 cups cold, cooked meat (chicken, beef, veal, or lamb), chopped
2 cups meat stock
1 cup canned tomatoes
2 medium onions
1 tablespoon Worcestershire sauce
salt and pepper, to taste
2 tablespoons butter or margarine
1/2 cup rice

Cook the meat, which has been cut into cubes, stock, tomatoes, one of the onions cut fine, Worcestershire sauce, and seasonings together for about 10 minutes. Melt the butter in a frying pan and add the onion and uncooked rice. Allow both to brown slightly and add them to the other mixture. Turn all into a buttered casserole and bake at 350° for 40 minutes.

Meat Croquettes

2 cups ground cooked meat
1 teaspoon onion, finely chopped
salt and pepper
1 cup thick white sauce (see page 31)
1 egg
1 tablespoon water
fine dry bread crumbs

Mix meat and onion and season to taste with salt and pepper. Combine with white sauce. Chill mixture thoroughly, then divide evenly into separate portions, allowing 2 tablespoons for each croquette. Shape into balls, cylinders, cones, or any desired shape. Beat egg with 1 tablespoon of water. Roll the croquettes in crumbs, dip in egg, again roll in crumbs, and fry in oil until light brown in color. Drain on paper towels.

Stuffed Pork Chops

6 double chops with pockets
3/4 cup raisins
1/2 cup celery, chopped
1/2 cup green bell pepper, chopped
2 tablespoons onion, minced
1 cup apple, chopped
3 cups soft bread crumbs
salt and pepper

Brown chops, stuff with the above ingredients, and put extra stuffing on top. Cover and bake at 350° for 1-1/2 hours.

Golden Fried Pork Chops

pork chops
salt and pepper, to taste
1 egg
1/2 cup evaporated milk
all-purpose flour
lard or shortening

Wash pork chops and salt to taste. Mix together the egg and evaporated milk in a mixing bowl. Dip each pork chop in the egg mixture, then batter with flour. Fry in lard or shortening.

Barbecued Lamb Shanks

4 lamb shanks
salt and pepper
2 cups water
2 cups cooked rice
1/2 cup chili sauce
1 tablespoon vinegar
1 tablespoon Worcestershire sauce
1/4 cup water

Season the lamb shanks with salt and pepper. Cover with water and simmer until tender for about 1-1/2 hours. Remove the meat from the bones. Place the rice in a greased baking dish, lay the meat on the rice. Cook together chili sauce, vinegar, Worcestershire sauce, and water. Pour the mixture over the meat and rice. Bake at 350° for about 30 minutes.

Lamb Shoulder Chops with Dressing

5 shoulder arm or blade lamb chops
2 teaspoons bacon drippings
3 cups coarse, dry bread crumbs
1/2 cup cold water
1 medium onion, grated
2 tablespoons parsley, chopped
1/2 to 1 teaspoon poultry seasoning
1/2 teaspoon salt
1 egg
5 slices bacon

Brown chops slowly in bacon drippings. Meanwhile, soak crumbs in the water until all water is absorbed. Squeeze out any excess. Sprinkle onion, parsley, and seasoning over crumbs. Add beaten egg and mix lightly to distribute well. Put dressing in bottom of a buttered baking dish. Cover with the browned chops. Cover dish and bake at 325° for about 1 hour. Remove cover. Place a slice of bacon on each chop and bake 15 minutes longer to crisp bacon. Makes 5 servings.

POULTRY

Frosted Chicken Royale

1 teaspoon gelatin
1 tablespoon cold water
1 tablespoon hot water
1 can chicken
1/2 cup small cooked peas
1/2 cup sweet pickle, minced
1/4 cup pimento, minced
1/2 cup cream, whipped

Soak gelatin in cold water; dissolve in hot water. Add to chicken, peas, pickles, and pimento. Mix well. Fold in whipped cream. Freeze slightly (or merely chill thoroughly) in single tray. Makes 4 servings.

Barbecued Chicken

1 whole chicken, cut in half
salt and pepper, to taste
4 tablespoons butter, divided
2 tablespoons brown sugar
1/8 teaspoon allspice
1 tablespoon vinegar
1/8 teaspoon cloves
1 teaspoon mustard
dash of cayenne pepper
1/4 cup Worcestershire sauce
juice and rind of half of 1 lemon

Season chicken with salt and pepper and dot with 1 tablespoon butter. Broil until chicken is about half done. Combine remaining ingredients and cook over low heat for 7 to 10 minutes until thoroughly blended. When chicken is half done, begin basting with sauce. Turn chicken and baste again. Continue until chicken is done and tender.

Herbed Chicken and Potatoes

1 pound potatoes, thinly sliced
8 lemon slices
4 chicken breast halves, with bone
1 envelope herb with garlic soup mix
1/3 cup water
1 tablespoon olive oil

Combine potatoes and lemon slices in a baking or roasting pan. Place chicken on top. Combine soup mix, water, and oil in a bowl and pour over chicken and potatoes. Bake at 375° for 50 minutes, uncovered, or until chicken is done and potatoes are tender.

Oven Fried Chicken

1 (2 to 3-pound) chicken
1 cup flour
1 teaspoon salt
1/4 teaspoon pepper
1 teaspoon paprika
1/2 cup butter

Cut chicken into serving pieces, then wash and drain. Put flour, salt, pepper, and paprika in a paper bag. Place chicken in bag and shake well to coat each piece with seasoned flour. Melt butter in a large baking pan. Place chicken, skin side down, in pan. Bake at 425° for 30 minutes. Turn each piece of chicken and bake for 15 more minutes.

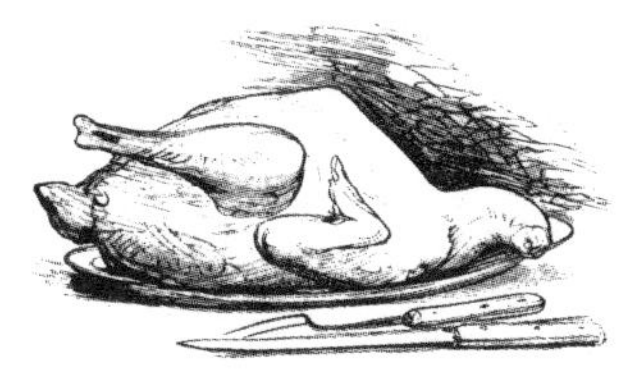

Chicken Breasts with New Potatoes

1/4 cup butter
4 to 6 large chicken breasts
1 onion, sliced
1 garlic clove, minced
2 tablespoons flour
1/2 teaspoon salt
1/4 teaspoon pepper
1 chicken bouillon cube
1 cup hot water
6 small new potatoes, boiled

Melt butter in a large skillet and sauté chicken on both sides until brown. Remove chicken. Add onion and garlic and cook about 5 minutes. Add flour, salt, and pepper. Return chicken to skillet. Dissolve bouillon cube in hot water and slowly pour over browned chicken. Cover and cook on low heat for about 25 minutes or until chicken is tender. Add new potatoes. Makes 4 to 6 servings.

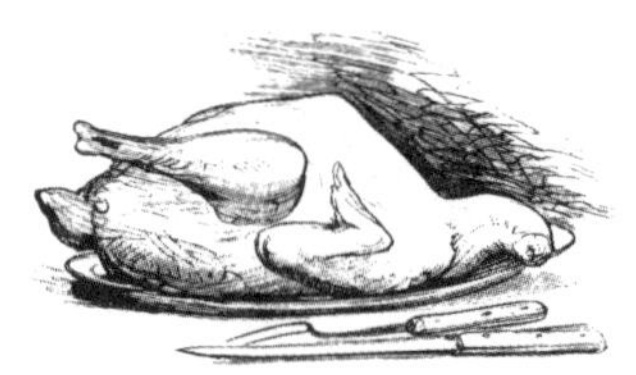

Chicken Tetrazzini

1-1/2 cups spaghetti noodles
1-1/2 cups celery, diced
1 tablespoon green bell pepper, chopped
1/2 cup onion, chopped
1 garlic clove, minced
1 tablespoon parsley, grated
chicken broth
2 cups chicken, cooked and diced
1/2 can condensed mushroom soup
3/4 cup canned tomatoes, drained
salt and pepper, to taste
3/4 cup sharp cheese, grated
2 tablespoons bread crumbs

Cook noodles, celery, bell pepper, onion, garlic, and parsley in chicken broth. Combine noodle mixture, chicken, mushroom soup, tomatoes, salt, and pepper in a casserole. Add cheese and bread crumbs on top. Bake at 300° until browned slightly.

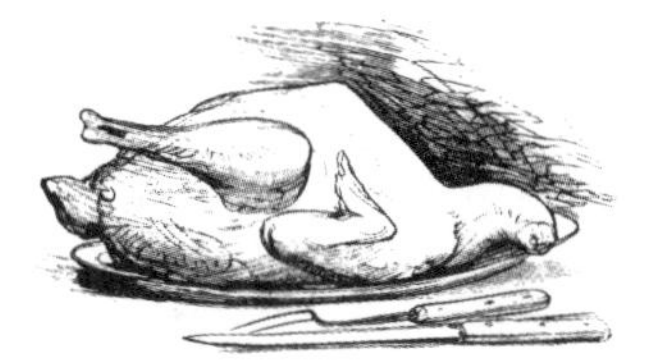

Chicken Cacciatore

1 frying chicken, cut into serving pieces
1/4 cup olive oil
1 medium onion, finely chopped
1 green bell pepper, finely chopped
1 red bell pepper, minced
1 garlic clove, minced
2 tomatoes, peeled and chopped
1 small can sliced mushrooms
1 teaspoon salt
1 tablespoon dried parsley
dash of pepper
1/4 teaspoon dried oregano
1/8 teaspoon allspice
2 cups tomato sauce
1/2 pound spaghetti noodles, cooked

Rinse chicken and drain. Brown chicken in hot oil and remove from pan. Add onion, peppers, and garlic. Cook, stirring frequently. Add the remaining ingredients except noodles and stir to blend well. Add the chicken, cover and simmer for 35 to 45 minutes or until chicken is tender. Place the chicken in the center of a platter and arrange spaghetti around the outside. Spoon the sauce over the chicken and spaghetti. Makes 3 to 4 servings.

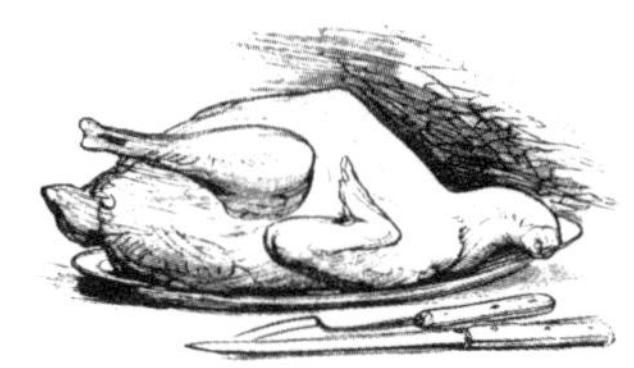

Chicken Dressing

2 cups cornbread crumbs
2 cups biscuit crumbs
1 small onion, finely chopped
1/2 teaspoon sage
1-1/2 cups chicken, cooked and roughly chopped
1-1/2 cups chicken broth
2 tablespoons parsley, chopped
1 teaspoon poultry seasoning

Combine all ingredients in a pan and mix well. Bake at 350° for about 1 hour. Add more broth if stuffing becomes too dry.

Southern Fried Chicken

2 to 3 pounds chicken pieces
salt and pepper, to taste
2 eggs, well beaten
4 cups flour
2 teaspoons garlic powder
1 teaspoon paprika
vegetable oil, for frying

Rinse the chicken and pat dry. Season each piece with salt and pepper, then dip in eggs. Dredge in flour, which has been seasoned with garlic powder and paprika, then fry in hot oil until golden brown.

Chicken Spaghetti

3 bell peppers, chopped
1 stalk celery, chopped
4 medium onions, chopped
1 garlic clove, minced
1 tablespoon olive oil
1 whole chicken, boiled, meat removed and cut into small pieces
2 tablespoons chili powder
1 box spaghetti noodles, cooked
1 can mushroom soup
1 large can mushrooms
1 small can pimentos
1 pound grated cheese

In a large saucepan, sauté the bell peppers, celery, onions, and garlic in olive oil. Add the rest of the ingredients and stir well. Pour into a casserole and bake at 400° for about 45 minutes.

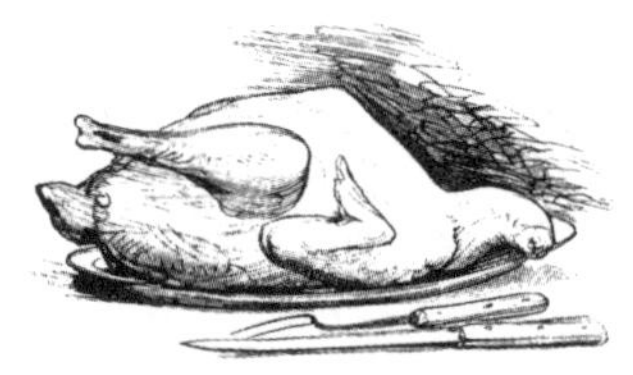

SEAFOOD

Fish Baked with Stuffing

2 cups soft bread crumbs
1/4 cup melted butter margarine
1/2 teaspoon salt
1 tablespoon onion, grated
1 tablespoon parsley, chopped
1/4 cup cold water
1 whole fish like haddock or whitefish

Combine the first six ingredients in the order given. If a dry stuffing is preferred, the water may be omitted. Clean and wipe the fish. Rub the inside with additional salt. Fill it with stuffing and sew together. Brush the outside of the fish with additional melted butter. Bake at 375° for about 15 minutes to the pound.

Codfish Balls

1 cup salted codfish
3 cups potatoes, diced
1 egg
1/2 teaspoon butter or margarine
1/8 teaspoon pepper
bread crumbs
oil

Soak the codfish in cold water overnight. Drain and shred. Cook potatoes and codfish together until potatoes are tender. Mash, add the egg, butter, and pepper. Beat until light. Shape into cakes, roll in fine, dry bread crumbs, and pan fry until browned on both sides.

Scalloped Flaked Cod

1 pound flaked cod
1-1/2 cups white sauce (see page 31)
1/4 cup buttered crumbs

Arrange the fish and sauce in layers in a well-greased baking dish. Cover with bread crumbs. Bake at 350° until heated throughout and the crumbs are browned on top. Any kind of cooked fish may be flaked and prepared in this way. This recipe is suitable also for canned salmon or tuna fish.

Salmon Loaf

1 cup flaked, cooked salmon, or canned salmon
1 cup bread crumbs
1/2 cup milk
1 teaspoon salt
1 tablespoon butter or margarine
1/2 teaspoon onion juice
1 egg yolk, beaten
1 teaspoon lemon juice
1 egg white, stiffly beaten

Combine the ingredients in the order given, folding in the stiffly beaten egg white last. Place the mixture in a well-greased pan and bake in a moderately hot oven or steam the mixture. Other cooked fish like cod, halibut, or haddock may be used in place of salmon.

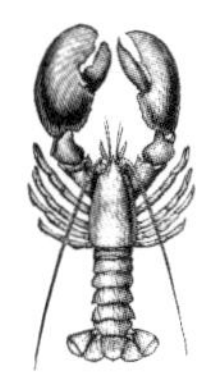

Scalloped Oysters

1 quart oysters
4 tablespoons butter or margarine
1/4 cup flour
1 cup milk
1 cup oyster liquor
1 teaspoon salt
1/8 teaspoon pepper
soft bread crumbs

Remove the oysters from the liquor, and pick them over carefully to remove any pieces of the shell. Strain the liquor. Melt the butter, add the flour, add the milk and oyster liquor. Season. Put alternate layers of oysters and sauce in a greased baking dish. Cover with crumbs, dot with butter. Bake at 375° until heated through and the crumbs are browned.

Shrimp Creole

1 onion, minced
2 garlic cloves, minced
2 tablespoons oil
1 pound shrimp, rinsed and deveined
1 bay leaf
1/2 small bell pepper
1 can tomato paste
2/3 cup water
hot cooked rice

Sauté onions and garlic in cooking oil until they turn yellow. Add shrimp and cook a few minutes longer, turning and stirring often. Add remaining ingredients and simmer for 1 hour. Serve on hot rice.

Shrimp Remoulade

1/2 cup tarragon vinegar
1 tablespoon horseradish-mustard
1 teaspoon salt
1/2 teaspoon cayenne pepper
1 tablespoon paprika
2 tablespoons ketchup
1 garlic clove, crushed
1 cup vegetable oil
1/2 cup green onion, minced
1/2 cup celery, minced
2 pounds shrimp, cooked and cleaned

Mix vinegar, mustard, salt, pepper, paprika, ketchup, and garlic. Add oil and beat well. Add green onions and celery. Pour over shrimp and let stand in refrigerator for at least 1 hour.

Fish Baked in Milk

2 tablespoons butter
1-1/2 pounds fish fillets
1 teaspoon salt
2/3 cup water
2/3 cup evaporated milk

Melt butter in a pan. Place fish on top of melted butter and sprinkle with salt. Add water and milk. Bake at 350° until fish is tender, about 45 minutes. Makes 6 servings.

Salmon Casserole

2 cups canned salmon, drained and flaked
1 cup English peas, cooked
1 cup milk
2 tablespoons butter
2 tablespoons quick-cooking tapioca
1 tablespoon onion, minced
1/2 teaspoon salt
1/4 teaspoon pepper
1/4 teaspoon paprika
biscuit dough (see page 39)

Combine all ingredients, except biscuit dough, in the order listed. Mix well, turn into greased casserole and bake at 400° for about 25 minutes. Roll out biscuit dough to 1/4-inch thickness. Stir contents of casserole and place dough on top. Bake 15 more minutes.

Creamed Salmon

1/3 cup milk
1 (10-1/2-ounce) can condensed cream of mushroom soup
2 cans salmon
1/2 teaspoon Worcestershire sauce

Combine milk and mushroom soup; stir until blended. Flake salmon and add to mushroom mixture. Season with Worcestershire sauce. Serve on hot toast.

Oven Fried Oysters

1 dozen large oysters
1 cup flour
1 teaspoon salt
1/4 teaspoon pepper
1 egg, slightly beaten
bread crumbs
salad oil

Roll oysters in flour seasoned with salt and pepper. Dip in the egg and roll in bread crumbs. Dip in salad oil and place in a shallow pan. Bake at 400° for 30 minutes, or until brown. Serve with tartar sauce and slices of lemon.

Salmon Croquettes

1 large can salmon, drained and flaked
1/2 cup buttermilk
1/4 teaspoon baking soda
2 cups cracker crumbs
4 eggs

Combine all ingredients and form into patties. Fry in hot oil until brown. Makes about 12 croquettes.

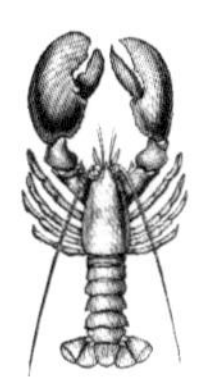

Tuna Fish Loaf

1 (7-ounce) can tuna fish
1/2 cup dry bread crumbs
2 tablespoons green bell pepper, finely chopped
1/2 cup celery, diced
1 tablespoon onion, diced
3 eggs, beaten
1 (11-ounce) can condensed vegetarian vegetable soup, undiluted
3 green bell pepper rings
1 egg, hard-boiled and sliced

Combine first seven ingredients. Grease a loaf pan and arrange bell pepper rings in bottom. Place a slice of hard-boiled egg in center of each ring. Pack loaf mixture in pan. Bake at 350° for 45 to 60 minutes or until firm.

Seafood Casserole

1 cup shrimp, cooked
1 cup crab meat
1 cup green peas, cooked
1/2 teaspoon salt
1/8 teaspoon pepper
2 tablespoons onion, chopped
1 green bell pepper, chopped
1 cup celery, diced
1-1/2 cups brown rice, cooked
1 teaspoon Worcestershire sauce
1-1/8 cups mayonnaise
3/4 cup whole wheat bread crumbs

Combine all ingredients in a casserole, reserving some bread crumbs for topping. Bake at 350° for about 30 minutes.

CAKES

Buttermilk Pound Cake

2 cups sugar
1 cup butter
3 cups flour
1/2 teaspoon baking soda
1/2 teaspoon baking powder
1 cup buttermilk
4 eggs, unbeaten
1 teaspoon vanilla extract
1 teaspoon lemon juice
1 teaspoon salt

Cream together sugar and butter. Sift together the flour, baking soda, and baking powder. Add milk to sugar mixture, then alternate one egg at a time with dry ingredients. Add vanilla and lemon juice. Beat this mixture about 3 minutes. Pour batter into a cake pan and bake at 300° for 1-1/2 hours.

Date Nut Cake

1 cup dates, chopped
1 cup water
2-1/2 cups flour, sifted
1 teaspoon baking powder
1 teaspoon baking soda
1 teaspoon salt
1/2 cup vegetable oil
1 cup buttermilk
1/2 teaspoon vanilla
1/2 cup nuts, chopped
3 eggs
1-1/2 cups sugar

Cover dates with water and cook until tender. Drain and cool. Sift together flour, baking powder, baking soda, and salt. Add vegetable oil, buttermilk, and vanilla. Beat until it forms a very smooth batter, then add dates and nuts and mix well. In a separate bowl, beat the eggs until thick and foamy. Gradually add sugar and continue beating until well blended. Fold the eggs and sugar mixture thoroughly into batter and bake in two 9-inch pans for 35 to 40 minutes.

Coconut Cake

3 cups flour, sifted
2 cups sugar
1 teaspoon salt
3/4 cup shortening, melted
1-1/2 cup milk, divided
5 teaspoons baking powder
3 egg yolks plus one whole egg
1 teaspoon vanilla
1 large coconut
3 egg whites
1 cup sugar
6 tablespoons white corn syrup

Sift together flour, 2 cups sugar, and salt. Add shortening and 1 cup of milk; stir until moist. Beat with an electric mixer for 2 minutes. Stir in baking powder, 3 egg yolks and 1 whole egg, 1/2 cup of milk, and vanilla. Beat 2 more minutes in electric mixer. Pour batter into prepared pans. Bake at 350° for 30 to 35 minutes.

Pour the milk from the coconut and place it in the oven to heat before cracking, about 15 to 20 minutes. Grate coconut.

For frosting, beat together 3 egg whites, 1 cup of sugar, and white corn syrup in top of a double boiler. Beat constantly until frosting stands in soft mounds, 3 to 4 minutes. Remove from heat and beat until peaks stand on top, about 1 minute. Let cake cool before stacking. Take the coconut milk and divide it into 3 equal parts. As you stack the cake, spoon milk gently on top of each layer and spread frosting on top of moist cake, then spread layer of the fresh grated coconut on each layer.

Strawberry Refrigerator Cake

1 (15-ounce) can condensed milk
1/4 cup lemon juice
1 cup sliced strawberries
2 egg whites, stiffly beaten*
24 vanilla wafers

Blend the condensed milk and lemon juice. Stir until the mixture thickens. Add sliced strawberries. Fold in stiffly beaten egg whites. Line a narrow, oblong pan or spring-form cake pan with waxed paper. Cover with some of the strawberry mixture. Add a layer of vanilla wafers, alternating in this way until the strawberry mixture is used, and finishing with a layer of wafers. Chill in the refrigerator for 6 hours or longer. To serve, turn out on a small platter and carefully remove the waxed paper. Cut in slices and serve plain or with crushed sweetened strawberries. Makes 8 servings.

Brown Betty

3 tablespoons melted butter or margarine
2 cups bread crumbs
4 apples, sliced or diced
1/3 cup sugar
1 teaspoon grated lemon or orange rind
1/2 cup water or fruit juice

Pour melted butter or margarine over crumbs and mix well. Cover the bottom of a greased baking dish with half of the crumbs. Place a layer of apples on top. Cover with one half the sugar and lemon or orange rind. Add another layer of crumbs. Cover with the remaining apples, sugar, and lemon rind. Add water to moisten. (It may be fruit juice alone or fruit juice and water.) Bake at 375° until the apples are tender, 35 to 40 minutes. Serve hot or cold with milk, cream, hard sauce, or soft custard.

*See page 178 for information about cooking with raw eggs.

Chocolate Ice Box Cake

30 ladyfingers
2 cakes sweet chocolate
3 tablespoons evaporated milk, undiluted
4 eggs, separated*
3 tablespoons sugar
2 cups evaporated milk, whipped

Line a mold or cake pan with ladyfingers. Melt chocolate in double boiler, adding milk, sugar, and beaten yolks of eggs. Cook slowly until thick and smooth, stirring constantly. When this is cool, fold it into the stiffly beaten egg whites. Place this filling in the cake form and set in refrigerator several hours. Cover with whipped evaporated milk at serving time. Alternate layers of lady fingers and filling may be used in any style pan. Garnish with strawberries or any other fruit.

Pound Cake

1/2 pound butter
1-3/4 cups sugar
5 eggs
pinch of salt
2 cups flour, sifted
1 teaspoon vanilla

Cream butter and sugar thoroughly. Add eggs, one at a time, beating well after each addition. Add salt, then flour gradually, beating well. Add vanilla and bake in greased loaf or tub cake pan at 325° for 1 hour and 45 minutes, or until cake leaves sides of pan.

*See page 178 for information about cooking with raw eggs.

Applesauce Cake

2 cups sugar
1 teaspoon salt
2 eggs
3 cups unsweetened apples, dried
1 pound dates
1 pound candied cherries
4 cups flour
1 tablespoon vanilla
1 tablespoon cinnamon
1 large box white raisins
2 cups nuts
2 cups fig preserves
2 teaspoons baking soda, dissolved in 2 tablespoons hot water

Combine all ingredients in a thick pan and cook on low heat. Place a pan of water over cake while cooking. Dump cake on plate and wrap in wax paper; cover plate. Let steam for 1-1/2 hours.

Pecan Cake

6 eggs, separated
1-1/2 cups sugar
2 teaspoons baking powder
2 tablespoons cake flour
3 cups pecans, finely chopped
2 cups whipping cream
1 teaspoon vanilla
1/4 cup powdered sugar

Beat egg yolks and sugar until foamy. Mix baking powder, flour, and nuts with stiffly beaten egg whites and fold this mixture lightly into the sugar and egg yolk mixture. Pour into pans lined with wax paper and well greased. Bake at 350° for 15 to 20 minutes. Let cool in pans.

Mix whipped cream with vanilla and powdered sugar. Spread over top of cakes.

Banana Cake

1/4 cup shortening
1 cup sugar
1 egg
1 cup very ripe bananas, mashed
1 cup nuts
1-1/2 cups flour
1 teaspoon baking soda
1 teaspoon vanilla
1 cup raisins

Cream shortening and sugar. Add egg and mashed bananas. Add remaining ingredients. Put in a greased pan and bake at 350° until done.

Angel Food Cake

1 cup cake flour, sifted
1-1/2 cups sugar, divided
2 eggs, separated
1/4 teaspoon salt
1-1/4 teaspoon cream of tartar
1 teaspoon vanilla
1/4 teaspoon almond extract

Sift flour and 1/2 cup sugar. Place egg whites and salt in a large bowl and beat until foamy. Add cream of tartar and beat until stiff enough to hold up definite peaks, but not dry. Continue beating, adding remaining sugar rapidly, one tablespoon at a time. Beat only until sugar is blended.

Add flavoring, then sift in dry ingredients, a small amount at a time, folding each addition with a wire whisk. Turn into a greased 10-inch tube pan. Bake at 350° for 30 to 35 minutes. Invert pan until cake is cold.

Devil's Food Cake

1/4 cup shortening
1 cup sugar
2-1/2 ounces unsweetened chocolate
1/2 cup sweet potatoes, mashed
1 egg, separated
6 tablespoons milk
1-1/4 cups flour
2 tablespoons baking powder
1/2 cup nuts, chopped
1/2 teaspoon vanilla
1/2 cup raisins

Cream shortening, add sugar, melted chocolate, and mashed potatoes. Mix well. Add egg yolk, milk, flour, and baking powder. Beat well and add nuts, vanilla, raisins, and egg white. Mix thoroughly. Put batter into a well greased pan and bake at 350° for 25 to 30 minutes.

Fruit Cake

1/2 pound butter
2 cups sugar
4 whole eggs, separated
1 cup milk
3 cups flour
2 teaspoons baking powder
1/4 pound candied cherries
1/2 pound canned coconut
2 rings candied pineapple
1 pound pecans
1/2 pound white raisins

Cream butter and sugar together thoroughly. Beat in egg yolks. Then add milk and flour (sifted with baking powder) alternately, reserving a little flour to dredge over fruit. Add candied cherries and coconut. Flour remaining fruit and nuts and add.

Add the beaten egg whites. Line a tube pan with greased brown paper. Pour batter into pan and bake at 275° for 2-1/2 to 3 hours, or until done.

Pineapple Upside Down Cake

3/4 cup cake flour, sifted
1/4 teaspoon salt
1 teaspoon baking powder
3 egg yolks
1/2 cup sugar
1/4 cup boiling water
1/2 teaspoon lemon juice
6 tablespoons butter
6 tablespoons brown sugar
1 can sliced pineapple, drained
candied cherries

Sift together flour, salt, and baking powder. Beat egg yolks until thick and light. Continue beating and add sugar gradually, about one minute longer. Add hot water and lemon juice, mix a few seconds to blend. Add flour a little at a time while continuing to mix slowly and scraping sides of the bowl frequently with a rubber spatula. Set aside.

Melt brown sugar and butter in a frying pan. Place pineapple slices on bottom of pan and place a candied cherry in the center of each slice. Pour batter on top and bake at 350° for 25 to 30 minutes. Makes 8 servings.

Refrigerator Icing

2 eggs
4 squares bitter chocolate
4 tablespoons warm milk
2 cups confectioner's sugar
1/2 teaspoon vanilla
dash of salt
6 tablespoons melted butter

Beat eggs until golden and thick in double boiler. Melt chocolate over hot water; add milk; mix to smooth paste. Pour over eggs. Add sugar gradually, stirring constantly. Let remain in double boiler and beat for 15 minutes, then add butter slowly. Store in covered jar in refrigerator.

Frosting

1/2 cup corn syrup or honey
1/2 cup sugar
2 egg whites*
1/4 teaspoon salt
1/2 teaspoon vanilla extract

Cook the syrup and sugar together until the mixture spins a thread. Stir constantly. Beat the egg whites until frothy. Add the salt and beat until stiff. Pour syrup slowly over the egg whites. Beat until the frosting stands in peaks. Add vanilla extract. Beat it until stiff enough to spread.

To make chocolate frosting, use the above recipe. After the frosting has been beaten stiff, add 3 squares of chocolate, melted, and blend thoroughly.

*See page 178 for information about cooking with raw eggs.

Seven-Minute Frosting

2 egg whites
1-1/2 cups sugar
5 tablespoons cold water
1-1/2 teaspoons light corn syrup
1 teaspoon vanilla

Put the egg whites (unbeaten), sugar, water, and corn syrup in the upper part of the double boiler. Place it over rapidly boiling water, beat constantly, and cook 7 minutes or until the frosting will stand in peaks. Remove from heat, add vanilla, and beat until thick enough to spread.

Creamy Peanut Butter Frosting

2 tablespoons peanut butter
1-1/3 cups sweetened condensed milk
1/8 teaspoon salt

Measure the peanut butter and condensed milk into the top part of a double boiler. Cook over boiling water until the mixture thickens, about 5 minutes, stirring all the while. Add the salt, cool, and spread on a cold cake.

Cream Filling

1/4 cup sugar
1 tablespoon flour
1/8 teaspoon salt
1 egg
1 cup milk
1/2 teaspoon vanilla

Combine the dry ingredients. Add the egg, slightly beaten, and mix well. Add the milk. Cook in a double boiler for about 15 minutes, stirring constantly, until the mixture thickens. Cool and add the vanilla.

Orange Marmalade Cake

3 cups flour, sifted
4 teaspoons baking powder
1/2 teaspoon salt
3/4 cup shortening
1-3/4 cups sugar
3 eggs, well beaten
1/2 cup orange juice
1 teaspoon lemon juice
grated rind of 1 orange
1/2 cup water
orange marmalade

Sift flour, baking powder, and salt together. Cream shortening with sugar until fluffy. Add eggs and beat thoroughly, then add juices, orange rind, and water. Add sifted dry ingredients and beat well. Pour into three greased pans and bake at 350° for 30 minutes. Cool, spread orange marmalade between layers.

Cup Cakes

1/2 cup shortening
2 cups brown sugar
1/2 cup peanut butter
1 cup hard cereal
1/2 teaspoon salt
3 eggs
2 cups flour
3 teaspoons baking powder
1 cup milk

Cream together the shortening, brown sugar, and peanut butter. Add the cereal, salt, and eggs. Mix thoroughly. Sift together the flour and baking powder. Add dry ingredients to first mixture alternately with milk. Bake in paper baking cups at 350° for 30 minutes. Top with your favorite frosting.

COOKIES

Golden Glow Cookies

1/2 cup butter
1 cup sugar
2 eggs
zest of 1 lemon
zest of 1 orange
2 tablespoons orange juice
2 tablespoons lemon juice
3 cups flour
1 teaspoon baking powder
1/4 teaspoon soda
1/2 teaspoon salt

Cream butter, work in the sugar gradually; cream thoroughly. Add beaten eggs; beat vigorously. Add grated rinds and juices. Add dry ingredients sifted together. Mix well. Shape into long rolls about 2 inches in diameter. Wrap in wax paper. Chill. Slice cookies paper thin; bake on greased cookie sheet at 375° for 10 to 12 minutes.

Oatmeal Cookies

1/4 cup raisins
1/3 cup flour
1 teaspoon baking powder
1/8 teaspoon soda
1/4 teaspoon salt
1/4 cup sugar
1/3 cup molasses
1 egg
1 tablespoon milk
1/4 cup melted shortening
1-1/4 cups oatmeal
1/2 tablespoon grated lemon rind

Wash the raisins and drain. Mix and sift the flour, baking powder, soda, and salt. Combine the sugar, molasses, beaten egg, and milk with melted shortening, and mix well. Add flour and oatmeal gradually. Add raisins and grated lemon rind. Drop from a teaspoon on greased baking sheets. Bake at 375° from 12 to 15 minutes. Makes about 3 dozen cookies.

Chocolate Chip Cookies

1/2 cup shortening
1/3 cup honey
1 egg, beaten well
2 tablespoons water
1 cup flour
1 teaspoon baking powder
1/4 teaspoon salt
1/2 teaspoon cinnamon
1/2 teaspoon allspice
1/2 cup chocolate chips
1/2 teaspoon vanilla
1/2 cup nuts, chopped

Cream the shortening; add the honey, and blend well. Add the egg and water, and beat well. Add the flour, baking powder, salt, and spices which have been mixed and sifted. Stir in chocolate chips, vanilla, and nuts. Drop by tablespoonfuls on a greased baking sheet. Bake at 375° from 10 to 12 minutes. Makes about 4 dozen cookies.

Molasses Ginger Hermits

1/2 cup shortening
1/2 cup sugar
1 egg, beaten
1 cup molasses
3 cups flour
1/2 teaspoon soda
3 teaspoons baking powder
1 teaspoon ginger
1 teaspoon salt
1/4 cup sour milk
1 cup raisins

Cream together the shortening and sugar. Combine the egg and molasses and mix thoroughly. Sift together the flour, soda, baking powder, ginger, and salt. Add to the creamed mixture alternately with sour milk. Add raisins. Drop by teaspoonfuls on a greased baking sheet. Bake at 400° for about 10 minutes. Makes 7-1/2 dozen 2-inch cookies.

Fudgies

1/4 cup shortening
1/2 cup sugar
1/2 cup dark corn syrup
1 teaspoon vanilla extract
1 egg
2 squares chocolate, melted
2 cups flour
1/2 teaspoon soda
1 teaspoon salt
1/2 cup buttermilk or sour milk
3/4 cup nuts, chopped

Cream together the shortening and sugar. Add syrup gradually, beating after each addition. Blend in vanilla extract. Add the egg and beat until light. Add melted chocolate. Sift together the flour, soda, and salt. Add to the creamed mixture alternately with buttermilk, beating smooth after each addition. Add nuts. Drop by teaspoonfuls on greased baking sheets. Bake at 350° from 10 to 15 minutes.

Ginger Snaps

1/2 cup butter
1 cup brown sugar
1 cup molasses
6 cups sifted flour
1 teaspoon ginger
1 teaspoon baking soda
1 teaspoon salt
1/2 cup hot water

Cream butter and brown sugar. Beat in molasses. Sift flour with other dry ingredients. Add molasses mixture alternately with water. Knead well and roll thin. Cut and bake on a greased cookie sheet at 350° for 8 to 10 minutes.

Peanut Butter Honey Cookies

3/4 cup raisins
2-1/2 cups flour
1-1/2 teaspoons baking powder
1/4 teaspoon soda
1/2 teaspoon salt
1/2 cup shortening
1/2 cup peanut butter
1/2 cup honey
1/2 cup brown sugar
1 egg
1/2 teaspoon vanilla

Wash the raisins and drain. Sift the flour with baking powder, soda, and salt. Cream the shortening and peanut butter together, blending them well. Add the honey, mixing it in thoroughly. Add the sugar gradually, blending it in. Add the egg and beat. Add vanilla. Stir in the dry ingredients slowly. Shape into a roll. Wrap in waxed paper, chill thoroughly. Cut in thin slices and bake at 400° for about 10 minutes. Makes 5 dozen cookies.

Caramel Nut Slices

1 cup butter
2 cups brown sugar
2 eggs
3-1/2 cups flour
1/2 teaspoon salt
1 teaspoon baking soda
1 cup pecans, chopped

Mix butter, sugar, and eggs thoroughly. Sift flour, salt, and baking soda. Blend in pecans. Combine wet and dry ingredients. Form two rolls, 2 inches in diameter, and wrap with wax paper. Chill in refrigerator 8 hours. Cut in slices 1/8-inch thick. Place on ungreased cookie sheet and bake at 400° for 10 to 15 minutes. Makes about 12 dozen cookies.

Bridge Cookies

1 cup butter, softened
1/2 cup sugar
1 egg
1 tablespoon vanilla
3 cups flour, sifted
1/2 teaspoon baking soda

Mix butter, sugar, egg, and vanilla thoroughly. Sift flour and baking soda and add to wet ingredients. Mix to form dough. Roll thin and cut with cookie-cutter. Bake at 400° for 10 to 15 minutes. Makes 6 dozen cookies.

Pecan Doubles

1 cup flour
1 cup butter
1/2 cup sugar
2 eggs, well beaten
1 cup brown sugar
1 teaspoon baking powder
1 cup pecans

Mix flour, butter, and sugar, and pack into a baking pan. Bake at 350° for 10 minutes. Mix eggs, brown sugar, baking powder, and pecans thoroughly; pour on top of the first mixture and bake 20 minutes or until firm. Cut the cookies into squares.

Nut Cookies

3 tablespoons cocoa
1/2 cup vegetable oil
2 eggs
1 cup sugar
1 teaspoon vanilla
3/4 cup self-rising flour
1 cup nuts, chopped

Combine all ingredients. Bake in greased square pan at 365° for 40 minutes. Cook in pan and cut into squares. Makes 2 dozen cookies.

Butterscotch Thumbprints

1/2 cup butter
1/4 cup brown sugar
1 egg, separated
1/2 teaspoon vanilla
1 cup self-rising flour, sifted
nuts, finely chopped
jelly

Mix butter, brown sugar, egg yolk, and vanilla. Stir in flour. Roll 1 teaspoon dough into balls. Dip in beaten egg whites and roll in finely chopped nuts. Place on baking sheet and press thumb in center of each. Bake at 350° for 10 to 12 minutes. Fill cooled thumbprints with jelly. Makes 3 dozen cookies.

Old-fashioned Teacakes

1/2 cup butter
3 cups sugar
3 eggs
3 cups flour
2 tablespoons baking powder
1 cup milk
1 teaspoon vanilla

Mix butter, sugar, and eggs together; combine dry ingredients and add alternately with milk and vanilla. Roll to about 1/4-inch thickness and cut with a cookie-cutter. Bake at 375° until brown.

Pineapple Drop Cookies

2 cups flour, sifted
1/2 teaspoon baking powder
1/4 teaspoon baking soda
1 teaspoon salt
2/3 cup shortening
1-1/4 cups brown sugar, firmly packed
2 eggs
3/4 cup crushed pineapple, drained
1 teaspoon vanilla

Sift flour with baking powder, soda, and salt. Cream shortening and add sugar gradually. Cream together until light and fluffy. Add eggs one at a time, beating well after each. Add pineapple and vanilla. Add flour a small amount at a time, beating after each addition until smooth. Drop from teaspoon on ungreased baking sheet. Bake at 400° for 10 minutes or until done. Makes about 4 dozen cookies.

Molasses Pecan Cookies

1/2 cup shortening
1/2 cup sugar
2 eggs
1/2 cup molasses
1-1/2 cup all-purpose flour, sifted
1-1/4 teaspoon baking soda
1/4 teaspoon mace
1/4 teaspoon salt
1 cup pecans, finely chopped

Cream together shortening and sugar; add eggs one at a time, beating after each. Add molasses and mix well. Sift together flour, baking soda, mace, and salt and add 1/2 cup pecans; mix well. Gradually add to creamed mixture. Drop by teaspoon on greased baking sheet, 2 inches apart; sprinkle top with remaining nuts. Bake at 350° for about 12 minutes. Remove from pan immediately. Makes 4 dozen cookies.

Praline Cookies

3 tablespoons butter
1 cup brown sugar, firmly packed
1 egg
1 cup pecan halves
4 tablespoons flour
1 teaspoon vanilla

Melt butter and stir in sugar; mix well. Add beaten egg, nuts, flour, and vanilla. Drop from a teaspoon onto a greased cookie sheet about 5 inches apart. Bake at 350° for 8 to 10 minutes. Let cool 1 minute before removing from cookie sheet with spatula. Makes about 5 dozen cookies.

Dream Bars

1/2 cup butter, softened
1-1/2 cup brown sugar, divided
1 cup plus 2 tablespoons flour
2 eggs
1 teaspoon vanilla
1/4 teaspoon salt
1/2 teaspoon baking powder
1 can moist pack coconut
1 cup pecans, chopped

Cream together butter, 1/2 cup sugar, and 1 cup flour until crumbly. Pat out into a greased pan. Bake at 350° for 20 minutes.

Beat eggs, add vanilla and remaining cup sugar with 2 tablespoons flour, salt, and baking powder, mix well. Add coconut and pecans. Pour over baked mixture. Return to oven and bake for 30 more minutes. Cool 5 minutes. Cut into 2 x 1-inch bars. Makes 3 dozen cookies.

Brown Sugar Cookies

1 cup butter
2 cups brown sugar
2 eggs
1/2 cup buttermilk
3-1/2 cups flour
1 tablespoon baking soda
1 tablespoon salt
nuts or chocolate chips (optional)

Cream together butter, brown sugar, and eggs. Stir in buttermilk and mix thoroughly. Sift flour, baking soda, and salt together. Add to creamed mixture with nuts or chocolate chips, if desired, and allow to chill for 1 hour. Drop by teaspoon onto a lightly-greased cookie sheet 2 inches apart. Bake at 350° for 8 to 10 minutes.

Oatmeal Drop Cakes

1 cup shortening
1-1/4 cups sugar
2 eggs
1 cup raisins
2 cups rolled oats
1 cup flour
2 teaspoons cinnamon
1/4 teaspoon baking soda
5 tablespoons milk

Cream shortening and sugar together. Add beaten eggs and raisins. Add rolled oats mixed with flour. Add cinnamon, soda, and milk; mix thoroughly into a stiff batter. Drop by teaspoons on a greased cookie sheet. Bake at 350° for 10 to 12 minutes.

Cinnamon Candy Cookies

1/2 pound butter
1 cup sugar
1 egg, separated
2 cups flour, sifted
1 teaspoon cinnamon
colored candies

Cream together butter and sugar thoroughly. Beat in egg yolk and add flour and cinnamon; blend well. Roll pieces of dough into 1-inch balls. Place balls on an ungreased cookie sheet about 2 inches apart. Press paper thin with a spatula. Paint with egg white and sprinkle with colored candies. Bake at 350° for 10 to 12 minutes. Makes 6 dozen.

Carnival Cookies

1 cup shortening
1-1/2 cups brown sugar
3 cups flour, sifted
1/2 teaspoon salt
1/2 teaspoon baking soda
2 eggs
2 teaspoons vanilla
2 cups peanuts
granulated sugar

Cream shortening and brown sugar. Sift flour, salt, and soda together. Add eggs, vanilla, and sifted dry ingredients. Stir in peanuts. Shape into balls the size of a walnut. Place 2 inches apart on an ungreased cookie sheet. Flatten with a spatula. Sprinkle sugar over cookies. Bake at 350° for 12 to 15 minutes. Makes about 5-1/2 dozen.

Sugar Cookies

5 cups cake flour, sifted
2 teaspoons baking powder
1/2 teaspoon salt
1 teaspoon baking soda
1 cup shortening
1 cup sugar
2 eggs, beaten
1 teaspoon vanilla
1 cup sour cream

Sift flour, baking powder, salt, and soda together. Cream shortening and sugar. Add eggs and vanilla. Beat well. Add sifted ingredients alternately with cream in small amounts. Chill. Roll about 1/4-inch thick. Sprinkle with additional sugar and cut with large cookie cutter. Bake at 375° for about 20 minutes. Makes 3 dozen cookies.

Frozen Cookies

1 cup brown sugar
1 cup white sugar
3/4 cup butter
1 cup vegetable shortening
3 eggs, well beaten
1 teaspoon salt
1 teaspoon baking soda
1 teaspoon cinnamon
1 teaspoon cloves

Cream sugars, butter, and shortening together. Add the eggs and beat well. Sift together the remaining ingredients and add to egg mixture. Work dough into a long round roll and wrap it with plastic wrap. Freeze for 3 hours. Slice thin and place on a cookie sheet. Bake at 400° for 7 minutes.

PIES
OUR
BEST

Apple Pie

5 sour apples
1/2 cup sugar, or 1/4 cup sugar and 1/4 cup honey
1/4 teaspoon cinnamon
1/8 teaspoon nutmeg
1 teaspoon butter or margarine

Make pastry for a two-crust pie (see page 149). Line the pie plate with pastry. Pare, core, and slice the apples and fill the pie. Sprinkle sugar or sugar and honey, cinnamon, and nutmeg over the apples. Dot over with butter. Wet the edges of the undercrust and cover with the upper crust, pressing the edges close together. Bake at 425° until the crust is brown, then 350° until the fruit is cooked. Other fruits, such as berries, cherries, peaches, or rhubarb, may be used in place of apples.

Lemon Meringue Pie

1 can sweetened condensed milk
1/2 cup lemon juice
grated rind of 1 lemon, or 1 teaspoon lemon extract
2 eggs, separated
1 baked pie shell
4 tablespoons granulated sugar

Blend together condensed milk, lemon juice, grated lemon rind or lemon extract, and egg yolks. Pour into a baked pie shell. Cover with meringue made by beating egg whites until stiff and adding sugar. Bake at 325° from 20 to 25 minutes, or until brown. Allow it to cool before serving.

Lemon Meringue Pie №2

2 tablespoons cornstarch, or 4 tablespoons flour
1 cup sugar
1/4 teaspoon salt
2 eggs, separated
1-1/4 cups water
juice of 1 lemon
grated rind of 1 lemon
1 baked pie shell
2 tablespoons sugar

Mix the cornstarch or flour, sugar, and salt, and combine with beaten egg yolks. Add water and cook in a double boiler, stirring constantly until the mixture is thickened and smooth. Just before removing from the heat, add lemon juice and rind. Cool slightly. Pour into a baked pie shell.

Beat egg whites stiff and add 2 tablespoons sugar, beating it in thoroughly. Cover with meringue and bake at 350° until the meringue is browned, or for about 15 minutes.

Lemon Chiffon Pie

1 tablespoon gelatin
1/4 cup water
4 eggs, separated*
1 cup sugar, divided
1/2 cup lemon juice
1 teaspoon grated rind
baked pie shell
whipping cream

Soak gelatin in cold water. Beat egg yolks until light, then add 1/2 of the sugar, lemon juice, and rind. When very light, place on low heat and cook, stirring until of custard consistency. Add soaked gelatin and dissolve. Cool. When cool add beaten egg whites to which the remaining sugar has been added. Fill baked pie shell and chill. Serve with thin layer of whipped cream.

Million Dollar Pie

1 (15-ounce) can sweetened condensed milk
1/2 cup lemon juice
1 (20-ounce) can fruit cocktail, drained
1/2 cup chopped pecans
1 (9-ounce) container frozen whipped topping, partially thawed
2 (9-inch) graham-cracker crusts

Mix milk, lemon juice, and drained fruit in a medium bowl. Fold in pecans and partially thawed whipped topping. Pile half of mixture into each crust. Chill an hour or more, until firm.

*See page 178 for information about cooking with raw eggs.

Raisin Pie

1-1/2 cups raisins
1-1/2 cups boiling water
1 tablespoon flour
1/2 cup sugar
1 tablespoon lemon juice
grated rind of 1/2 lemon
1/2 cup walnuts, finely chopped (optional)
double-crust pastry (page 149)

Wash the raisins carefully. Cook in the boiling water until plump. Add flour and sugar, mixed; cook a few minutes until the mixture thickens. Cool. Add lemon juice, rind, and chopped walnuts. Pour in a pie tin, lined with pastry. Cover with pastry. Bake at 450° for 35 or 40 minutes. Reduce the heat to 350° during the last 10 minutes.

Pumpkin Pie

1-1/4 cups mashed pumpkin
1/4 cup sugar
1/2 teaspoon cinnamon
1/4 teaspoon ginger
1/8 teaspoon cloves
1/2 teaspoon salt
1 egg, slightly beaten
1 cup milk
single-crust pastry (page 149)

Mix the ingredients in the order given. Bake in a pie pan lined with pastry at 450° until the crust is set, or for about 15 minutes, then 350° until firm, for about 20 minutes longer.

CHERRY TART

1 can cherries, pitted
1/2 cup sugar
1 tablespoon cornstarch
juice of 1/2 lemon
cream filling (page 109)
1 baked pie shell

Drain the juice from the canned cherries. Cook the juice and sugar together until the quantity is reduced to 1 cup. Add cornstarch and cook until clear and thickened. Add lemon juice. Cool slightly. Place a layer of cream filling in the bottom of the pie shell. Cool. Add drained and pitted cherries. Pour juice over the cherries. Chill.

Pastry mixture may be baked in individual tarts and the same produce used for filling.

PINEAPPLE CHIFFON PIE

1 tablespoon gelatin
1/4 cup cold water
4 eggs, separated
1/2 cup sugar, divided
1-1/4 cups canned, crushed pineapple
1 tablespoon lemon juice
1/4 teaspoon salt
baked pie shell

Soak gelatin in cold water about five minutes. Beat egg yolks slightly and add 1/4 cup sugar, pineapple, lemon juice, and salt. Cook on low heat until it reaches custard consistency. Add the softened gelatin, stirring thoroughly, and cool. When mixture begins to thicken, fold in stiffly beaten egg whites to which has been added the other 1/4 cup sugar. Fill baked pie shell and chill. Just before serving, spread a thin layer of whipped cream over pie.

Refrigerator Chocolate Pie

1 cup milk
1/2 cup sugar
3 egg yolks
1/4 teaspoon salt
2 squares chocolate, melted
1/2 tablespoon gelatin, soaked in 1/4 cup cold water
3 egg whites, beaten
1/4 cup sugar
1-1/2 cups vanilla wafer crumbs or cake crumbs
1 cup cream, whipped

Combine first five ingredients in top of a double-boiler; cook and stir over gently simmering water until desired consistency is reached. Add soaked gelatin and dissolve. Cool. Fold in beaten egg whites, add the 1/4 cup sugar. Line a buttered pie tin with vanilla wafer crumbs; add filling. Cover with waxed paper and place in refrigerator 4 to 5 hours. Serve with whipped cream.

Egg Custard Pie

2-1/3 cups milk
3 eggs, beaten
1/2 cup sugar
1/4 teaspoon salt
1/4 teaspoon nutmeg
1 (9-inch) pie shell

Combine all ingredients and pour into the pie shell. Bake at 375° for 25 minutes.

Strawberry Cream Pie

1 cup sugar
6 tablespoons cornstarch
1/2 teaspoon salt
2-1/2 cups milk, scalded
2 eggs, slightly beaten
3 tablespoons butter
1/2 teaspoon vanilla
1 (9-inch) baked pastry shell
1 pint strawberries, sliced
1 cup heavy cream, whipped

Mix sugar, cornstarch, and salt; gradually add milk and cook in double boiler until thick. Add small amount of hot mixture to eggs; stir into remaining hot mixture. Cook until thick, stirring constantly. Remove from heat; add butter and vanilla. Pour into cooled baked shell. Chill. Cover with strawberries. Chill, spread with sweetened whipped cream just before serving. Garnish with halved berries.

Orange Pecan Pie

1 cup sugar
1 teaspoon salt
1 tablespoon flour
1 cup dark corn syrup
3 eggs, beaten until foamy
1/2 cup orange juice
1 tablespoon orange zest
1-1/2 cups pecans, crumbled
single-crust pastry (page 149)

Mix sugar, salt, and flour. Add syrup, eggs, orange juice, and zest. Stir in pecans, pour into a pastry lined pie pan. Bake at 400° for about 10 minutes, reduce heat to 350°. Bake about 30 minutes, or until pastry is brown.

Pineapple Cream Pie

1/2 lemon rind, grated
3/4 cup sugar
3/4 cup flour, sifted
1/4 teaspoon salt
1/2 cup milk
1-1/2 cups crushed pineapple, drained, juice reserved
3 egg yolks
3 tablespoons butter
juice of half of a lemon
1 (9-inch) baked pie shell

Mix grated lemon rind with sugar, flour, and salt. Gradually add the milk, stirring until the mixture is smooth. Add pineapple juice and cook over boiling water in top of a double boiler, stirring constantly until thick. Beat yolks until foamy. Add cream filling in a thin stream very slowly, stirring constantly. Return mixture to double boiler and cook another 5 minutes, stirring constantly. Stir in butter until it melts; take off stove and stir in lemon juice and cool. When cold, stir in crushed pineapple and pour into pie shell.

Banana Pie

2 cups milk
2/3 cups sugar
1/3 cup flour
1/2 teaspoon salt
2 eggs
1 teaspoon vanilla
1 tablespoon butter
3 medium ripe bananas
1 (9-inch) baked pie shell
whipped cream

Scald milk in top of a double boiler; mix together sugar, flour, and salt. Add this mixture gradually to milk; cook over boiling water, stirring constantly, until thick. In a small bowl, beat eggs slightly. Gradually stir in a small amount of hot mixture, then quickly pour back into double boiler and cook 3 minutes. Remove from heat and add vanilla and butter. Slice the bananas and put into pie shell, reserving half of one banana. Pour filling over bananas and let it cool two or three hours. When ready to serve, swirl one cup whipped cream over pie and top with remaining banana slices.

Apple Crumble Pie

1/3 cup flour
3/4 cup brown sugar, firmly packed
1/3 cup butter
6 medium tart apples, pared and sliced

Combine flour and brown sugar; cut in butter to make a crumbly mixture. Arrange sliced apples in bottom of a greased, shallow baking dish. Sprinkle sugar over the top and bake at 375° for about 30 minutes, or until top is golden brown and the apples are tender.

Chocolate Cream Pie

3 squares unsweetened chocolate
2-1/4 cups milk
1 cup sugar
4 tablespoons flour
1/4 teaspoon salt
2 egg yolks, slightly beaten
2 tablespoons butter
1 teaspoon vanilla
1 (9-inch) pie shell
2 egg whites
4 tablespoons sugar

Add chocolate to milk and heat in double boiler. When chocolate is melted, beat until blended with milk. Combine sugar, flour, and salt; add gradually to chocolate mixture and cook until thickened, stirring constantly. Continue cooking for 10 more minutes. Pour small amount of mixture over egg yolks, stirring vigorously. Return to double boiler and cook 2 minutes longer. Remove from heat; add butter and vanilla and let cool. Pour into pie shell. In a mixing bowl, beat egg whites until foamy; add sugar 2 tablespoons at a time, beating after each addition until sugar is blended. Continue beating until mixture will stand in peaks. Pile lightly on filling, bake at 350° for 15 minutes.

Lemon Cake Pie

1 cup sugar
1 tablespoon butter
2 eggs, separated
juice and zest of 1 lemon
2 tablespoons flour
2 cups milk
1 (9-inch) pie shell

Cream sugar, butter, and egg yolks; add lemon juice and zest, then flour and milk. Beat well. Fold in stiffly beaten egg whites and pour into pie shell. Bake at 450° for 10 minutes. Reduce heat to 350° and bake for 25 minutes more.

Strawberry Pie

1/4 cup sugar
3 tablespoons cornstarch
1 pint frozen strawberries, thawed
1 (8-ounce) package cream cheese
1 (9-inch) baked pastry shell
whipped cream

Mix sugar, cornstarch, and syrup from strawberries. Cook over low heat, stirring constantly until thick. Add strawberries and cool.

Spread cream cheese on baked pastry shell. Pour in strawberry mixture and top with whipped cream.

Coconut Custard Pie

4 eggs
2/3 cups sugar
1/2 teaspoon salt
1 cup shredded coconut
2-2/3 cups milk
1 teaspoon vanilla
1 (9-inch) pie shell

In a large mixing bowl, beat eggs slightly. Slowly mix in remaining ingredients except pie shell, reserving a small portion of the coconut for topping. Pour mixture into pie shell and bake at 450° for 15 minutes, then reduce the heat to 350° and bake until the custard is set, about 20 minutes.

Cherry Pie

2 cans unsweetened cherries
4 tablespoons cornstarch
1 cup sugar
1 tablespoon butter
1/4 teaspoon salt
1 (9-inch) baked pie shell
whipped cream

Drain cherries, reserving the juice. Combine the cornstarch and sugar; add to cherry juice. Cook until clear and thick and remove from heat. Add butter, salt, and cherries, stirring carefully to prevent crushing cherries. Cool. Pour into pie shell and top with whipped cream.

Peach Pie

1/2 cup flour, sifted
1 cup sugar
1/2 cup margarine, melted
1/2 cup milk
1/2 teaspoon baking powder
2 eggs, beaten well
1/4 teaspoon salt
1 can peaches, drained

Mix together all ingredients except peaches in order given. Place peaches in a greased casserole and pour flour mixture on top. Bake at 350° until crust is light brown.

Marshmallow Pumpkin Pie

1/2 pound marshmallows
1 cup pumpkin, cooked
1/2 teaspoon cinnamon
1/4 teaspoon ginger
1/4 teaspoon salt
1 cup cream, whipped
1 (9-inch) baked pie shell

Place marshmallows, pumpkin, and seasoning on top of double boiler; stir until marshmallows are melted. Let cool at room temperature, and then stir in about one-third of the whipped cream into the pumpkin mixture. Pour into pie shell. Add remaining whipped cream on top and chill in refrigerator. Makes 6 servings.

Pecan Pie

1 cup corn syrup
1/2 cup sugar
4 tablespoons butter
3 eggs
1 teaspoon vanilla
1 (9-inch) pie shell
1 cup pecans

Mix corn syrup, sugar, and butter and cook until thick. Beat eggs until light. Pour the hot syrup over the eggs and heat well. Pour into pie shell. Cover with pecans and bake at 375° until the shell is well cooked.

Chess Pie

3 eggs
1 cup sugar
1 teaspoon vanilla
2 cups milk
1 (9-inch) pie shell

Mix eggs, sugar, vanilla, and milk thoroughly and pour into pie shell. Bake at 375° for about 40 minutes or until firm.

Black Bottom Pie

2 tablespoons unflavored gelatin
3 tablespoons cold water
1-1/2 cups milk
3 egg yolks
1/4 cup sugar
2 tablespoons cornstarch
2/3 cup semisweet chocolate
3/4 teaspoon vanilla
1 (9-inch) baked pie shell
3/4 teaspoon rum flavoring
whipped cream
shaved chocolate

Sprinkle gelatin over cold water. Heat milk until a film forms on top. Beat egg yolks until bubbles form; slowly stir in milk. Mix sugar and cornstarch together and add egg mixture. Place in top of a double boiler. Cook, stirring constantly, until mixture thickly coats a spoon. Measure 2/3 cup cooked custard into a bowl and add chocolate chips and vanilla. Beat until chocolate chips are well blended. Pour into pie shell, making a chocolate layer over entire crust. Chill. Stir softened gelatin into remaining custard, mix well. Chill for 20 to 30 minutes. Continue beating gelatin custard and add rum flavoring. Spoon over chocolate layer. Chill until firm. Garnish with whipped cream and shaved chocolate.

Frozen Lemon Pie

3 egg yolks, well beaten
1/4 cup lemon juice
1 teaspoon lemon zest
pinch of salt
1/2 cup plus 1 teaspoon sugar
1 cup heavy cream, whipped
3 egg whites, beaten stiff*
1 cup vanilla wafers, finely crushed

Combine the first five ingredients and cook until thick. Cool, fold in whipped cream and stiffly beaten egg whites. Sprinkle half of the wafer crumbs in ice tray. Pour over mixture and add remaining crumbs on top. Freeze until firm.

Butterscotch Pie

1 cup brown sugar
1/4 cup flour
1 cup milk
2 egg yolks, slightly beaten
4 tablespoons butter
1/2 teaspoon vanilla
1 (9-inch) baked pie shell
whipped cream

Place sugar and flour in top of double boiler. Add milk slowly and cook, stirring constantly until thickened. Add egg yolks and cook for 3 minutes. Remove from heat and add butter. When cool, add vanilla. Pour into pie shell and cover with whipped cream.

*See page 178 for information about cooking with raw eggs.

Angel Food Pie

1 cup crushed pineapple
1/2 cup water
1/2 cup sugar
1/8 teaspoon salt
2 tablespoons cornstarch, dissolved in cold water
2 egg whites, stiffly beaten*
1 (9-inch) baked pie shell
whipped cream
chopped nuts

Combine pineapple, water, sugar, and salt in a saucepan and heat until boiling. Add cornstarch. When thoroughly cooked, remove from heat and let cool. Fold in egg whites and pour into pie shell. Cover with whipped cream and sprinkle nuts on top. Chill in refrigerator.

Orange Pie

1-1/3 cup flour
1 cup sugar
1/4 teaspoon salt
juice and grated rind of 1 orange
juice of 1 lemon
2 tablespoons butter
3 egg yolks
1 (9-inch) baked piecrust

Mix together flour, sugar, salt, and grated rind. Add fruit juice and cook in double boiler until mixture thickens. Stir constantly. Add butter and beaten egg yolks. Cook 2 minutes longer. Pour into piecrust. Cover with meringue and brown in the oven.

*See page 178 for information about cooking with raw eggs.

Peanut Butter Pie

2 eggs, well beaten
1-1/2 cups milk
pinch of salt
3 tablespoons sugar
1/4 cup peanut butter
1 teaspoon vanilla
1 (9-inch) baked pie crust

Mix first five ingredients together and put in double boiler. Cook until thick; beat in 1 teaspoon of vanilla. Pour in pie crust. Chill.

Holiday Lime Pie

1 package lime-flavored gelatin
3/4 cup boiling water
1 small can evaporated milk, well chilled
1/2 cup sugar
2 tablespoons lime juice
green food coloring (optional)
1 cup heavy cream, whipped
1 (9-inch) baked pie shell
1 tablespoon sugar
fresh raspberries

Add gelatin to boiling water; stir until gelatin dissolves. Add milk, sugar, juice, and food coloring, if using. When cool and thickened, add 1/2 cup whipped cream. Pour into cold pie shell. Combine sugar and the remaining whipped cream. Spread on top of pie and arrange raspberries over top of cream. Chill in refrigerator until ready to serve.

Peach Cream Pie

1 (15-ounce) can sweetened condensed milk
1/4 cup lemon juice
1 cup diced canned peaches
1 graham cracker piecrust
2 egg whites
1/4 cup sugar

Blend condensed milk and lemon juice. Stir until mixture thickens. Fold in peaches and pour into pie shell. Beat egg whites until stiff. Add sugar and beat until mixed thoroughly. Pour on top of pie and bake at 350° until brown, about 10 to 15 minutes. Let pie stand at room temperature for 20 minutes. Then chill in refrigerator for 1 hour.

Blackberry Cream Pie

1-1/3 cups sweetened condensed milk
1/4 cup lemon juice
1-1/3 cup fresh blackberries
1 (9-inch) baked pastry shell
whipped cream

Combine condensed milk and lemon juice. Stir until mixture thickens. Fold in 1 cup of blackberries and pour into pastry shell. Cover with whipped cream and garnish with remaining blackberries. Chill.

Tropical Delight Pie

1 cup shredded coconut
1/4 cup butter
1-1/2 cups vanilla wafers, finely crushed
1 package orange-flavored gelatin
1 cup hot water
1/2 cup honey
2 tablespoons lemon juice
1 cup evaporated milk, chilled and whipped

Sauté coconut in butter, stirring constantly, until golden brown. Add wafer crumbs and mix well. Press half of the mixture in bottom of 9-inch pie pan.

Dissolve gelatin in hot water. Add honey and lemon juice. Chill until slightly thickened. Fold in whipped evaporated milk. Turn out over coconut crumb mixture in pan and top with remaining coconut crumbs. Chill until firm. Makes 8 servings.

Chocolate Chiffon Pie

1 tablespoon unflavored gelatin
1/4 cup cold milk
1/2 cup hot milk
2 ounces chocolate
4 eggs, separated*
1 cup sugar, divided
1/4 teaspoon salt
1 teaspoon vanilla
1 (9-inch) baked pie shell
whipped cream

Soften gelatin in cold milk, about 5 minutes. Combine hot milk and chocolate; stir until smooth. Add gelatin to chocolate mixture and stir until dissolved. Add slightly beaten egg yolks, 1/2 cup sugar, salt, and vanilla. Beat thoroughly, cool until mixture begins to thicken.

Beat egg white until foamy; beat in remaining sugar gradually and fold into gelatin mixture. Pour into pie shell and chill until firm. Spread whipped cream on pie before serving.

Graham Cracker Crust

18 graham crackers
1/4 cup sugar
1/3 cup butter

Crush graham crackers; add sugar and cut in butter. Press into a 9-inch pie plate to form crust. Bake at 375° for 8 minutes. Cool.

*See page 178 for information about cooking with raw eggs.

Two-crust Pie

2-1/4 cups flour
1 teaspoon salt
3/4 cup shortening
1/4 to 1/3 cup ice water

Sift the flour, measure, and sift again with salt. Add shortening and blend with flour, using two knives, a pastry blender, or finger tips, until the mixture resembles coarse cornmeal. Add water a little at a time until the mixture holds together when pressed with the fingers. Too much water makes tough pastry. Chill. For a two-crust pie, divide the dough into two pieces, allowing a little more for the bottom crust than for the top. Roll on a lightly-floured board, keeping the dough in a circular shape. Roll from the center toward the edges until the dough is about 1/8-inch thick. Fit into a pan allowing a border of about 3/4-inch to hang over the edges of the pan. Roll out the other half of dough, keeping it circular also and a littler larger than required to cover the top of the pan. Put the filling in the pan. Wet the edges with the fingers dipped in ice water. Lay rolled-out dough on top, press down around the edges of the pan, then flute two crusts together by pressing between the thumb and index finger or with the tines of a fork. Cut slits in the upper crust to allow steam to escape. The upper crust may be made of strips of dough arranged in lattice fashion. For fruit pies, a sprinkling of flour over the lower crust before adding the fruit will help to prevent juice from cooking out. Double crust pies usually require from 40 to 45 minutes of baking time. Bake in a hot oven, about 425°.

Single-crust Pies

For single-crust pies where the crust is baked before the filling is added, use one half of the recipe given above. Roll the dough and fit it over the outside of a pie tin. Flute the edges, prick with a fork to prevent air bubbles from forming during baking. Bake at 425° for about 20 minutes.

Pie Crust

2 cups all-purpose flour, sifted
1-1/2 teaspoons salt
1/2 cup vegetable oil
1/4 cup whole milk

Mix together dry and wet ingredients separately. Combine the wet ingredients into the dry. Stir lightly until mixed. Round up dough and divide in half. Place one half between 2 sheets of wax paper. Roll out gently until circle reaches the edges of the paper. Peel off top piece of paper. Place pastry in a 9-inch pie pan. Bake at 425° for about 10 minutes. Repeat with remaining half.

PUDDINGS

Old-fashioned Rice Pudding

1/4 cup rice
4 cups milk
1/4 teaspoon salt
1/3 cup sugar
1/2 teaspoon vanilla
grated rind of 1/2 lemon

Wash rice, mix with the other ingredients, and pour into a buttered pudding dish. Bake 3 hours at 250°, stirring three times during the first hour of baking to prevent the rice from settling.

Bread Pudding

4 cups bread cubes
4 cups milk
2 eggs
3/4 cup sugar
1/2 teaspoon salt
nutmeg

Soak bread cubes in milk; add beaten eggs, sugar, and salt. Pour into a greased pudding dish. Sprinkle the top sparingly with nutmeg. Place the pudding dish in a pan of hot water. Bake at 350° for about 30 minutes or until firm and brown on top. Makes 6 servings.

Banana Pudding

2 eggs, separated
2/3 cup sugar
1 tablespoon cornstarch, or 2 tablespoons flour
2 cups milk
1 teaspoon vanilla
2 or 3 bananas, sliced
15 graham crackers, crushed
1/4 cup sugar

Beat the egg yolks, add sugar and cornstarch or flour, and mix thoroughly. Add milk and cook in a double boiler until creamy, stirring constantly. Remove from the heat and add vanilla. Place graham crackers, sliced bananas, and custard in alternate layers in a baking dish. Add the custard. Beat the egg whites until stiff and add 1/4 cup sugar. Spread over the pudding and brown at 350°.

Chocolate Pudding

1 tall can evaporated milk
1/3 cup sugar
4 tablespoons cocoa
4 tablespoons cornstarch, or 8 tablespoons flour
1 teaspoon vanilla

Dilute the milk with an equal amount of water and scald. Mix sugar, cocoa, and cornstarch or flour; add scalded milk, and cook over hot water for 10 minutes, stirring constantly. Cool. Add flavoring. Serve cold.

Caramel Pudding

1-3/4 cups sugar (use brown, if on hand)
4 tablespoons cornstarch, or 8 tablespoons flour
3/4 teaspoon soda
2 tablespoons butter or margarine
1 tall can evaporated milk
1 teaspoon vanilla

Put the sugar, cornstarch or flour, soda, and butter in a skillet over low heat. Stir until the sugar is light brown and melted. Slowly add the milk, diluted with an equal quantity of water, and stir until thickened. Remove from heat; cool and add vanilla. Serve cold.

Corn Pudding

2 cups fresh corn cut from the cob
2 eggs, beaten
2 tablespoons melted butter or margarine
1 pint scalded milk
1 medium-sized green pepper, finely chopped
1 teaspoon salt
1/8 teaspoon pepper

Combine all ingredients. Pour into a greased baking dish. Set the dish in a pan of hot water. Bake at 350° until the pudding is firm, or for about 1 hour.

Frozen Marble Pudding

3 (3-ounce) packages chocolate snaps, crumbled
1 cup milk, scalded
1 cup cream, whipped
1 teaspoon almond extract
4 tablespoons powdered sugar
dash of salt

Pour scalded milk over crumbled wafers. Stir until smooth; cool. Place alternate layers of wafer mixture and whipped cream (sweetened and flavored) in deep tray; have top layer of cream. Freeze. Unmold on platter; serve sliced.

Baked Custard

2 eggs
2 tablespoons sugar
dash of salt
2 cups milk
nutmeg, to taste

Beat eggs slightly, add sugar, salt, and milk. Pour in custard cups and sprinkle with nutmeg. Place the cups in a pan of hot water and bake at 350° until the custards are firm and the mixture does not adhere to a knife when inserted.

Rennet Custard

1 rennet tablet
1 tablespoon cold water
3 tablespoons sugar
1 teaspoon vanilla
2 cups cold milk

Dissolve a rennet tablet by crushing it in cold water. Add sugar and vanilla to milk. Warm slowly, stirring constantly, until a drop is comfortably warm (not hot) on the wrist. Remove from heat. Add the dissolved rennet tablet and stir quickly for a few seconds only. Pour into individual dessert dishes. Allow it to stand undisturbed until firm, or for about 10 minutes. Chill. Makes 4 to 5 servings.

OTHER DESSERTS

Emerald Bavarian Cream

1 cup boiling water
1 package lime gelatin
1 cup chilled evaporated milk or cream for whipping
2 tablespoons lemon juice
pinch of salt
whipped cream

Pour boiling water over the gelatin and stir until dissolved. Chill. When beginning to set, whip until light and fluffy. Whip the evaporated milk or cream, add lemon juice and salt, and fold carefully into the whipped gelatin. Pour into dampened ring mold or individual molds and place in refrigerator to set until firm. Serve with whipped cream.

Vanilla Ice Cream

2 cups milk
3 yolks
3/4 cup sugar
1 cup cream, whipped
pinch of salt
1 tablespoon vanilla

Scald milk; pour over beaten egg yolks and sugar. Cook in double boiler until creamy-thick. Chill. Fold in whipped cream, salt, and vanilla. Freeze.

For chocolate variation: Melt 2 squares bitter chocolate in a little of the hot milk, over hot water. When thoroughly blended with milk, combine with sugar, egg yolks, and scalded milk and continue as for vanilla. May omit 1 or 2 egg yolks. Requires no stirring if watched closely.

Children's Special Frozen Delight

2 teaspoons gelatin
1/2 cup cold milk
2-1/2 cups milk, scalded
2 cup sugar
2 eggs, separated*
2 teaspoons flour
1 cup cream whipped
2 teaspoons vanilla (or 1-1/2 teaspoons almond)
pinch of salt

Soak gelatin 5 minutes in cold milk. Add to scalded milk in double boiler. Add sugar, flour, salt and 2 beaten egg yolks. Cook until like custard (about 10 minutes); stir often. Chill. Fold in 2 beaten egg whites; fold in whipped cream; add flavoring. Freeze. Beat with fork occasionally.

Marshmallow Ice Cream

20 marshmallows
1 cup sweet milk
1 cup cream, whipped
pinch of salt
1 tablespoon flavoring

Melt marshmallows (stale or fresh) with milk in double boiler. Chill. Beat thoroughly. Fold in the whipped cream. Add salt and vanilla, almond, or maple flavoring. Freeze without stirring. Makes 1 pint.

*See page 178 for information about cooking with raw eggs.

Chocolate Lover's Delight

1 tablespoon gelatin
1/4 cup cold water
1/4 cup boiling water
6 tablespoons cocoa (or 2 squares bitter chocolate)
1/2 teaspoon salt
3 eggs, separated*
1/2 cup granulated sugar
1 teaspoon vanilla
1/2 cup cream
1 cup whipped cream

Soak gelatin in cold water 5 minutes; dissolve in boiling water. Add cocoa (or melted chocolate). Add salt to egg whites; beat very stiff; add well-beaten yolks. Stir in the sugar, then add chocolate mixture, well-beaten. Beat all thoroughly. Add vanilla. Add thin cream; beat well; fold in whipped cream. Freeze. Makes 1 quart.

Banana Nut Cream

3 ripe bananas, mashed
3/4 cup confectioner's sugar
2 tablespoons lemon juice
pinch of salt
2 eggs whites*
1/2 to 1 cup chopped nuts
1 cup cream, whipped

Add sugar, lemon juice, and salt. Fold in stiff egg whites; then fold in whipped cream; add nuts. Freeze. Makes 1 quart.

*See page 178 for information about cooking with raw eggs.

Peppermint Candy Ice Cream

3/4 cup peppermint candy
1 cup water
2 egg whites*
1/8 teaspoon salt
1/8 teaspoon almond or vanilla extract
1-1/4 cups cream, whipped

Soak candy in the water. Heat very slowly until candy dissolves. Chill. Salt the egg whites; beat stiff. Fold in candy mixture. Add flavoring. Fold in whipped cream (or tall can evaporated milk whipped). Freeze. Serve with Chocolate Sauce (page 177).

Frozen Peach Fluff

12 marshmallows
1/2 cup peach juice
3 drops orange coloring
1/2 cup crushed peaches
3 egg whites, lightly beaten*
2 cups cream, whipped

Melt marshmallows in double boiler, with peach juice. Beat well. Cool and add coloring and peach pulp. Fold in beaten egg whites. Fold in whipped cream. Freeze. Beat mixture once hourly. Makes 1 quart.

Mocha Cream

2 cups coffee
1 cup condensed milk
2 squares bitter chocolate
dash of salt
1 cup cream

Cook coffee, condensed milk, and 2 squares bitter chocolate (previously melted over hot water) in a boiler until creamy and thick. Cool; add salt and fold in cream, whipped and well sweetened. Beat until creamy. Freeze.

Strawberry Marlow

1 pint strawberries
16 marshmallows
1 tablespoon lemon juice
1/2 pint cream

Crush finely or press through a sieve the washed, stemmed strawberries. Place the marshmallows in the top of a double boiler with two tablespoons of juice, and steam until melted. Stir until smooth, remove from stove, and add strawberries and lemon juice. Chill until mixture is cold and slightly stiffened; beat cream until stiff and lightly fold strawberry mixture into it. Freeze without stirring. Makes 6 servings.

Peach Marlow

1 cup fresh peaches, crushed
3 tablespoons sugar
20 marshmallows
1/4 cup water
1/2 pint cream

Sprinkle the crushed peaches with sugar and let stand while the marshmallows and water are steaming to the top of a double boiler. When marshmallows are just melted, add the sweetened peaches and cool. When cold and slightly stiffened, carefully combine with the cream, whipped stiff. Freeze without stirring. Makes 6 servings.

Standard Parfait

2/3 cup sugar
1/4 cup water
2 egg whites*
pinch of salt
2 tablespoons lemon juice
1 cup evaporated milk or cream
2 teaspoons vanilla

Cook sugar and water until it threads. Pour into the beaten egg whites, to which the salt has been added, beating constantly. Chill. Whip the evaporated milk or cream, add lemon juice, fold into the egg and syrup mixture, and add vanilla. Pour into freezing tray and freeze. Makes 8 servings.

*See page 178 for information about cooking with raw eggs.

Arabian Night's Parfait

1/2 cup dates, minced
1 cup water
1/2 cup orange juice
2 tablespoons lemon juice
4 eggs, separated*
1/4 teaspoon salt
1 cup cream, whipped
1/4 teaspoon vanilla

Cook dates in 1 cup water for 10 minutes, without stirring. Add fruit juices. Pour over well beaten egg yolks. Cook in double boiler for 15 minutes. Remove and cool. Salt the egg whites; beat stiff. Fold into date mixture. Fold in whipped cream; add vanilla. Freeze without stirring.

Praline Parfait

3/4 cup corn syrup
3 egg whites*
pinch of salt
2 cups cream, whipped
1 cup pecans or walnuts, crushed

Boil syrup until it spins a thread. Fold in very stiffly beaten egg whites. Add salt. Fold in whipped cream; add nuts. Freeze without stirring. Makes 1 quart.

*See page 178 for information about cooking with raw eggs.

Peanut Brittle Parfait

1 tablespoon butter
1/3 cup brown sugar
1/4 cup water
2 egg yolks
1-1/3 teaspoons vanilla
1 cup cream, whipped
1 cup peanut brittle, crushed

Cream butter and sugar; add water; cook until well blended, stirring. Beat egg yolks in double boiler until light; then add syrup slowly; beat until light and fluffy. Cool. Add vanilla to whipped cream; fold into cooked mixture, then add peanut brittle. Freeze. Makes 6 servings.

Blackberry Royal Parfait

2 cups blackberry juice and pulp
1 package lemon gelatin
1/4 cup of sugar
2 cups whipped cream
1 cup blackberries, whole

Heat blackberry juice and dissolve gelatin. Add sugar. Cool—turn into shallow pan and chill. When chilled, shred very fine with a fork, then add slightly sweetened whipped cream until a lavender color. To serve; add 1 tablespoon sweetened berries in bottom of parfait glasses, then lavender mixture, and top with whipped cream. Serve with crisp refrigerator cookies.

Butterscotch Mousse

1/2 cup brown sugar
2 tablespoons butter
6 tablespoons water
1 whole egg
1 egg yolk
2 tablespoons milk
1/2 teaspoon lemon juice
1 cup cream, whipped
pinch of salt

Bring sugar, butter, and water to boiling in saucepan. Beat whole egg and extra yolk in double boiler. Pour cooked mixture over eggs, stirring vigorously for smoothness. Add salt and milk. Cook 5 minutes, stirring constantly. Cool. Add lemon juice. Fold in whipped cream very gradually. Freeze. Makes 6 servings.

Chocolate Mousse

1 square bitter chocolate
1/4 cup milk
1/4 cup water
7 tablespoons sugar
2 egg yolks, beaten well*
pinch of salt
1/2 teaspoon vanilla
1 cup cream, whipped

Melt chocolate over hot water; heat the milk, water, and sugar to scalding point in double boiler; pour mixture over egg yolks, stirring vigorously; add mixture slowly to melted chocolate. Beat thoroughly. Add salt. Remove and cool. Fold into whipped cream (do not beat). Add vanilla. Freeze. Makes 6 servings.

*See page 178 for information about cooking with raw eggs.

Peach Mousse

2 cups fresh sliced peaches
2/3 cup sugar
2 cups cream, whipped
3 or 4 drops almond extract

Peel and slice peaches; cover with the sugar and let stand one hour. Mash and rub through a sieve. Fold in cream, whipped until stiff, and almond flavoring. Pour into ice tray. Freeze without stirring.

Floating Island

2 cups scalded milk
3 egg yolks
1/4 cup sugar
1/8 teaspoon salt
1 teaspoon vanilla
3 egg whites*
powdered sugar

Beat egg yolks slightly, add sugar and salt. Gradually add the scalded milk to the eggs, stirring constantly. Cook on low heat and continue stirring until mixture coats a spoon. Cool and add vanilla. Beat egg white until stiff, adding powdered sugar during last part of beating. Arrange this meringue on the custard. A little jelly, or rubyettes, may be placed in center of each "island." Floating Island should be served very cold.

Strawberry Bavarian Cream

2 tablespoons gelatin
1/4 cup cold water
1/2 cup fruit juice
1-1/2 cups crushed fresh strawberries
1-1/2 cups canned berries, drained
1-1/2 cups cream

Soak gelatin in cold water and dissolve in boiling fruit juice. Cool. If fresh fruit is to be used, sweeten to taste, depending upon the sweetness of the berries, about one-half cup; if canned fruit, no extra sugar will be needed. Add fruit and whipped cream and place in refrigerator to become firm. Unmold on serving plate and garnish with whole strawberries, crushed strawberries, or whipped cream, as desired.

Fruit Crème Sherbet

1 cup granulated sugar
1/2 cup water
1 whole egg
salt
pulp of 1 banana
juice of 1 orange
juice of 1-1/2 lemons
10 green cherries, minced
10 maraschino cherries, minced
1 cup cream, whipped
green food coloring

Boil sugar and water for 5 minutes. Pour over well beaten egg, stirring constantly. Salt the mashed banana; combine with fruit juices and egg-syrup mixture. Add cherries. Chill. Add coloring; fold in whipped cream. Freeze.

Pomelo Sherbet

1-1/2 cups sugar
3/4 cup light corn syrup
1-3/4 cups water
6 tablespoons lemon juice
3-3/4 cups grapefruit pulp

Cook sugar, syrup, and 1 cup of water to soft ball stage. Add remaining water and lemon juice. Cool. Dice grapefruit pulp; add pulp and juice to syrup. Freeze. Makes 2 quarts.

Pineapple Mint Sherbet

1/2 cup water
1 cup pineapple juice
1/2 cup sugar
1 teaspoon gelatin
1 cup crushed pineapple
1 tablespoon fresh mint, chopped
2 tablespoons lemon juice
2 egg whites*

Mix water, pineapple juice, and sugar. Boil three minutes. Add soaked gelatin and dissolve. Cool. Add crushed fruits, chopped mint, and lemon juice. Freeze for one hour. Turn into bowl, add unbeaten egg whites and beat until very light. Return to chilling unit and freeze.

*See page 178 for information about cooking with raw eggs.

Pineapple Cream Sherbet

1 cup sugar
2 cups boiling water
1-1/2 cups crushed pineapple
grated rind of one orange
1/2 cup lemon juice
1/2 cup orange juice
1/2 cup pineapple juice
1 cup cream, whipped
4 tablespoons powdered sugar
1 egg yolk, well beaten*
2 egg whites, beaten stiff*

Combine the sugar, water, pineapple, orange rind, and juices, then freeze to a mush. Combine the whipped cream, powdered sugar, egg yolk, and egg whites. Fold the two mixtures together thoroughly. Freeze until smooth and stiff.

Buttermilk Sherbet

2 cups buttermilk
1/2 cup sugar
1 cup crushed pineapple
1 egg white*
1-1/2 teaspoons vanilla

Combine buttermilk, sugar, and pineapple thoroughly. Place in an ice tray and freeze to a mush. Remove from tray to bowl, add egg white and vanilla. Beat until light and fluffy. Return to chilling unit and continue freezing.

*See page 178 for information about cooking with raw eggs.

Lemon Marshmallow Ice

24 marshmallows
1/2 cup water
1/2 cup lemon juice
1/8 teaspoon lemon zest
dash of salt
2 egg whites*

Melt the marshmallows with the water in top of a double boiler. When completely melted, remove from stove and add lemon juice, grated rind and salt. Turn into ice tray and freeze to mush. Beat the egg whites until stiff, stir the fruit mixture, and fold into the beaten whites. Return to the ice tray and continue freezing, stirring once when the mixture has again frozen to a mush. Makes 6 servings.

Lemon Sauce

1/2 cup sugar
1 tablespoon cornstarch, or 2 tablespoons flour
pinch of salt
1 cup boiling water
2 tablespoons butter or margarine
1-1/2 tablespoons lemon juice

Mix the sugar, cornstarch or flour, and salt. Add boiling water gradually, stirring constantly. Boil 5 minutes, remove from heat, add butter or margarine and lemon juice. Serve hot. Great with gingerbread.

MOCHA MIRACLE

1 tablespoon gelatin
2/3 cup milk
1/3 cup black coffee
3 eggs, separated*
1/2 cup sugar
pinch of salt
1 teaspoon vanilla
1 cup cream, whipped
27 vanilla wafers

Soak gelatin in a little milk. Heat milk and coffee in double boiler. Beat egg yolks, sugar and salt until thick. Add to hot mixture; cook, stirring constantly, until mixture coats a spoon. Add soaked gelatin; stir until dissolved. Remove from heat; add vanilla. When cooled slightly, pour over beaten egg whites. Beat well. When cold, fold in whipped cream. Place layer of wafers, about 9, on bottom of a square tin. Cover with mocha mixture. Repeat twice. Chill 24 hours. Cut in squares; remove with pancake turner. Serve with whipped cream.

FRUIT WHIP

1 cup fruit pulp (crushed berries, peaches, apple sauce, prune, or apricot pulp)
1 egg white*
1/4 cup powdered sugar

Put all the ingredients in a bowl together and beat until stiff for 10 to 15 minutes. Pile in sherbet glasses and chill.

*See page 178 for information about cooking with raw eggs.

Cranberry Crush

1 quart cranberries
3 cups boiling water
1 teaspoon baking soda
2 cups sugar
1/2 cup orange juice
1 tablespoon lemon juice

Cook cranberries in boiling water until berries burst. Stir in baking soda. Remove the greenish acid froth which will rise (use skimmer). Add sugar. Cook 10 minutes. Put through coarse sieve to remove skins. Add orange juice and lemon juice. Freeze.

Watermelon Sherbet

1 pint watermelon, diced
1/2 cup pineapple juice
juice of 1 lemon
1 cup maraschino cherries, undrained

To watermelon add pineapple juice, juice of 1 lemon, and maraschino cherries with syrup. Stir well. Freeze into soft sherbet.

Apricot Freeze

2 cups apricots
2 cups apricot juice
1 cup sugar
1 lemon

Mash apricot pulp and add apricot juice and sugar. Heat until sugar melts. Cool. Add juice and grated rind of 1 lemon. Freeze.

Lemon Sherbet

1/3 cup lemon juice, strained
1 cup confectioner's sugar
2 cups milk

Mix lemon juice with confectioner's sugar. Add milk very slowly. Stir well. Freeze with occasional stirring, if convenient.

Banana Sherbet

6 ripe bananas
1 cup sugar
2 cups water
juice of 1 orange
dash of salt

Mash pulp of bananas. Boil sugar with water for 5 minutes. Cool; add orange juice, and salt; combine with banana pulp. Freeze.

Spanish Cream

1 tablespoon gelatin
1/4 cup cold water
2 cups milk
2 eggs, separated*
1/3 cup sugar
1/8 teaspoon salt
1 teaspoon vanilla

Soften the gelatin in cold water. Scald the milk and add the gelatin, stirring until dissolved. Combine beaten egg yolks, sugar, and salt then slowly stir in the milk and gelatin mixture. Cook over hot water until slightly thickened, or for about 5 minutes. Cool. When the mixture begins to set, add vanilla and fold in stiffly beaten egg whites. Pour into one large, or six individual molds. Chill until set.

*See page 178 for information about cooking with raw eggs.

Doughnuts

1 egg
1 cup sugar
1 cup milk
pinch of salt
1 teaspoon baking powder
4-3/4 cups flour

Beat eggs well; add sugar and milk. Sift salt, baking powder, and flour together. Add egg mixture and stir to combine. Pour dough onto a well-floured board. Knead lightly and roll into 1/4-inch thickness. Cut with doughnut cutter and fry in hot oil. Drain.

Peanut Brittle

1-1/2 cups white sugar
2/3 cup light corn syrup
2 cups raw peanuts
1-1/2 teaspoons baking soda

Combine all ingredients except soda. Stir and cook 15 to 20 minutes or until nuts start popping and syrup turns dark. Remove from heat and stir in soda. Pour on a greased baking sheet and spread evenly. Cool.

Chocolate Sauce

1/2 cup cocoa
1/3 cup light corn syrup
3 tablespoons water
1-1/2 cups sugar
1/2 teaspoon salt
1 cup milk
3 tablespoons margarine
1/2 teaspoon vanilla

Mix together cocoa, corn syrup, and water. Cook over low heat until well blended. Stir in sugar, salt, and milk. Blend well and cook gently for about 10 minutes or until mixture starts to thicken. Remove from heat and add margarine. Beat a few minutes and stir in vanilla. Makes 2 cups.

*About Cooking with Raw Eggs

Many old-fashioned recipes, especially dessert recipes, call for raw eggs. As with all raw animal products, the consumption of raw eggs presents a very small risk of contamination by Salmonella bacteria, which can cause food poisoning. The risk is higher for people who are elderly, pregnant, very young, or have medical problems that affect the immune system. These people should avoid cooking with or eating any raw animal product.

The majority of us should use raw eggs carefully, as we would any raw animal product. Eggs should be refrigerated, clean and fresh, with unbroken shells. Use only grade AA or A eggs. After you have prepared recipes using the eggs, be sure to refrigerate uneaten portions within an hour. If you are making a recipe to travel on a picnic or to a gathering, or any time a dish using raw eggs will travel with you, be sure to use a cooler or other insulated container that will keep the dish at 40° or lower.

Egg whites are not a good medium for salmonella growth, but as an added safety measure, you might want to combine your egg whites with any sugar in the recipe (2 tablespoons per white) and beat over low heat until the whites make peaks. Then proceed with the recipe using the whites as called for. Raw yolks are at higher risk of bacterial contamination, so before using, you should cook them by combining the yolks with 2 tablespoons or less of the liquid in the recipe and cooking over low heat until the eggs coat a spoon. Then cool and use in the recipe.

Be sure to follow all good cooks' guidelines for cleanliness in the kitchen in everything you do, including washing hands and utensils thoroughly and keeping counters clean.

A

B

C

D

E

F

G

P

T

U

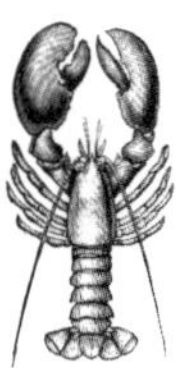

V

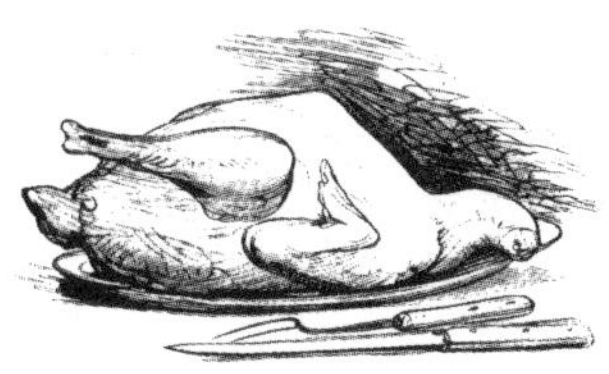